MARINSHIP AT WAR

Liberty ship heading out on Richardson Bay for a trial run.

MARINSHIP AT WAR

Shipbuilding and Social Change in Wartime Sausalito

CHARLES WOLLENBERG

FOREWORD BY JACK TRACY

WESTERN HERITAGE PRESS   Berkeley, California

Dedicated to the memory of Leah Levy Wollenberg.

Published by Western Heritage Press
P.O. Box 5108 Elmwood Station
Berkeley, CA 94705

Designed and produced by Dave Comstock. Composition by Comstock Bonanza Press and Dwan Typography. The typeface is Ehrhardt, designed in the 17th century by Nicholas Kis for the Erhardt foundry in Germany. Printed on recycled, acid-free paper by Thomson-Shore, Inc.

The publication of *Marinship at War* coincides with the opening of *Marinship 1942*1945*, a small museum at the U.S. Army Corps of Engineers Bay Model Visitors Center in Sausalito, California. We wish to thank the organizers of the Museum Project for allowing us to use materials from their collections. Readers of this book are urged to visit the San Francisco Bay Model exhibit, which is open to the public. All photographs are from the Sausalito Historical Society collection, and are reproduced with the permission of the society.

Library of Congress Cataloging-in-Publication Data

Wollenberg, Charles.
   Marinship at war : shipbuilding and social change in wartime Sausalito
/ Charles Wollenberg : foreword by Jack Tracy.
      p. cm.
   Includes index.
   ISBN 0-9621956-1-8 (alk. paper) : $8.95
   1. Marinship (Firm)—History. 2. Shipbuilding—California—Sausalito—History—20th century. 3. World War, 1939–1945—Social aspects—California—Sausalito. 4. Sausalito (Calif.)—Social conditions. 5. World War, 1939–1945—California—Sausalito. I. Title.
VM301.M363W65   1990
338.7'62383'0979462dc20

                                                          90-12512
                                                             CIP

Contents

Also by Charles Wollenberg

The Harvest Gypsies:
> *On the Road to* The Grapes of Wrath.
> Articles by John Steinbeck, collected and introduced
> by Charles Wollenberg. 1988.

Golden Gate Metropolis:
> *Perspectives on Bay Area History.* 1985.

All Deliberate Speed:
> *Segregation and Exclusion in California Schools, 1855–1975.* 1976.
> Updated paperback edition, 1978.

Neither Separate Nor Equal:
> *Race and Racism in California.* Coauthor and Editor. 1971.

Ethnic Conflict in California History
> Coauthor and Editor. 1970.

Preface

Very many people helped to make this book a reality. Cynthia Roby, coordinator of the Marinship museum project, gave generously of her time, knowledge and advice. Jack Tracy, president of the Sausalito Historical Society, was always a source of encouragement and opened his organization's collections to me. In particular, I was able to use the society's valuable Marinship oral history interviews, many of them conducted by Elizabeth Robinson, another important source of advice and support.

Martha Winnacker, Richard Walker, Jerry Herman, Harold and Jaqueline Wollenberg, Marilynn Johnson and Arthur Haskell read all or parts of the manuscript and gave good and necessary criticism. Paul Anderson also provided valuable counsel.

I received cooperation and assistance from the staffs of the Army Corps of Engineers San Francisco Bay Model, the Sausalito Public Library, the Bancroft Library and several other departments of the library of the University of California, Berkeley.

Last, but certainly not least, I am especially grateful to Harlan Kessel and Joe Engbeck of Western Heritage for their great commitment of time, energy and resources.

CHARLES WOLLENBERG

Foreword

Marinship was a hastily built wartime shipyard located on the formerly calm tidal marshes of Richardson Bay, just inside the entrance to San Francisco Bay from the Pacific Ocean. The yard was constructed in a time of both fear and courage, when American merchant ships were being destroyed in great numbers by German U-boats in the north Atlantic and when Japan had eliminated a major portion of the American fleet while it lay at anchor at Pearl Harbor on December 7, 1941.

To keep strong the supply lines to American forces, the United States Maritime Commission authorized the building of Marinship in Sausalito, California. The challenge to build the yard and to manage the record-breaking production of merchant vessels was accepted by the W. A. Bechtel Corporation.

This work documents the interaction of private enterprise, labor, and government in bringing into being 93 Liberty ships and tankers at Marinship. A work force of approximately 20,000 workers, men and women, were brought together from all over the country to do the job. Whether from the east, west, north or south, each contributed in his or her unique way to complete a task which made an enormous difference in the success of this country's war effort and which earned a heartfelt "Well done" from Vice Admiral Howard L. Vickery of the United States Maritime Commission.

This account of Marinship's role during World War II has been diligently researched by the author. He maintains a balance between historical fact and personal narrative in relation to the shipyard's influence on the social, economic, and political cycles of Sausalito, Marin County, and the San Francisco Bay Area both during and after the war. Marinship is no more, but the memories of those wartime years are still strong.

JACK TRACY
Founder and Director
Sausalito, March 1990   Sausalito Historical Society

CHAPTER ONE

World War II Comes to Pine Hill

IN THE EARLY 1890S, FRANCES Jackson moved into an eight-room house on a knoll overlooking the northern Sausalito waterfront in Marin County, across the Golden Gate from San Francisco. She and her husband planted the pine trees for which the hill was eventually named. A half-century later, the widowed Mrs. Jackson was still living in the house, and, at age 80, was the oldest resident of Pine Hill when she and her neighbors received an eviction notice. In early March 1942, they were told they had just two weeks to gather their belongings and leave. The homes of Frances Jackson and about thirty other families were going to be razed and Pine Hill leveled to accommodate Marinship, an emergency wartime shipyard owned by the United States Maritime Commission and operated by the W. A. Bechtel Company.

"It'll be hard to find another place," Mrs. Jackson observed, "but my friends are kind and I can live with them." Although the government was paying for their homes, some of Mrs. Jackson's neighbors were angry. Mrs. Hulsbrusch pointed to her magnificent garden: "Look," she said, "strawberries, artichokes, carrots, blackberries, blueberries ... all planted and watered. All this I have to leave on two weeks' notice." Another neighbor, Mrs. McLeod, had more practical concerns: "It's got to be done, I guess, but we'll never get our junk moved."[1]

Mrs. Jackson and the other residents of Pine Hill were about to be engulfed by the extraordinary tide of social and economic change produced by World War II. According to Gerald Nash, the major historian of the war's effect on the American West, World War II changed the region from an essentially "colonial" economy, based primarily on export and exploitation of raw materials, to a "diversified economy that included industrial and technological elements." Nash greatly underestimated the extent to which industrialization had already occurred in California before the war, but he was certainly correct when he argued that World War II brought a "great and cataclysmic" transformation to the West. The transformation was concentrated in California precisely because the state's economy was already well developed and had the potential for rapid expansion. California received nearly half of the $70 billion in federal funds allocated to the Far West from 1941 to 1945. With slightly over five percent of U.S. population, the state secured about 12 percent of the nation's defense contracts during the war years.[2] These contracts, concentrated in aircraft and ship construction, produced massive economic development and laid the foundation for California's postwar military-industrial complex, today by far the nation's largest.

The aircraft industry was located almost entirely in Southern California, while shipbuilding centered on San Francisco Bay. The Bay Area received three-quarters of all federal expenditures for ship construction on the West Coast during the war years, and the labor demands of local shipyards helped to produce a nine-county regional population increase of about 30 percent, or 500,000 people, between 1941 and 1945. The wartime shipbuilding boom changed Bay Area society more than any event since the California Gold Rush. Indeed, for the region, World War II is to the mid-twentieth century what the Gold Rush was to the mid-nineteenth: a profound historical watershed that transformed an entire era.[3]

The initial development of the Bay Area's maritime construction and repair industry was itself a product of the Gold Rush. San Francisco's first drydock was built in 1851, and the Navy established the Mare Island Shipyard at Vallejo in 1854. Subsequently, several additional repair and construction yards were built on the San Francisco waterfront, and by the end of the nineteenth century, similar enterprises also lined the shores of the Oakland Estuary. At the turn of the century, San Francisco's Union Iron Works was already producing major steamships, including the battleship *Oregon*. Local entrepreneurs owned most of the nineteenth-century yards, but in the early 1900s, Bethlehem Steel purchased Union Iron and its major competitor, the Ridson Iron Works, also located in San Francisco. World War I produced a short-term boom, but business declined with the cancellation of defense contracts in 1919 and fell even more drastically during the depression years of the early 1930s. By 1939, however, new federal expenditures for both military and civilian vessels were producing a modest recovery in Bay Area yards, and local shipbuilding employed about 6,000 workers.[4]

Five years later the figure was 244,000, a forty-fold increase. In 1944 the Bay Area alone had nearly six times the number of shipyard employees as had existed nation-wide in 1939. One-sixth of all wartime ship construction workers in the United States were employed in Bay Area facilities by 1944. Five billion dollars in defense contracts had made San Francisco Bay the largest shipbuilding center the world had ever seen.[5]

Much of the expansion occurred at existing enterprises such as the Bethlehem and Western Pipe yards in San Francisco, the Moore and Todd plants on the Oakland Estuary, and the naval yards at Mare Island and Hunters Point in San Francisco. But the region's largest wartime shipbuilding facility was a brand new enterprise—Henry Kaiser's vast Richmond complex. Kaiser-Richmond opened in 1941 and by 1944 employed more than 100,000 workers in four inter-connected shipyards.[6]

Marinship, like the Kaiser facility, was an "instant shipyard," built with incredible speed to meet the immediate national emergency. On March 2, 1942, Admiral Emory S. Land, Chairman of the U.S. Maritime Commission, wired Bechtel company headquarters in San Francisco, asking the corporation to submit a proposal for a new west coast shipyard. Bechtel responded within 24 hours with a tentative plan for a plant on the Sausalito waterfront, one of the few vacant industrial sites left along San Francisco Bay with good rail and highway access. A week later, Kenneth Bechtel and other company executives traveled to Washington with a detailed proposal. On March 12, just ten days after Admiral Land's initial request, Bechtel signed a Commission contract to build and operate the proposed facility and deliver 34 ships by the end of 1943.[7]

By April 1942, earth-moving equipment was tearing down Pine Hill, using it as fill to cover bayside marshes and tidelands and create a level site for the yard. More than 25,000 piles were driven to strengthen the fill, as plumbers laid vast networks of underground pipe for water, compressed air, acetylene and oxygen. A highway and the Northwestern Pacific rail line were relocated, and the Pacific Gas and Electric Company laid a new 11,000-volt power cable to accommodate the emerging industrial complex. Dredges carved a deep water channel from the

Northern Sausalito waterfront in March 1942 before Marinship construction. Pine Hill, soon to be demolished, is in the center.

Sausalito waterfront on Richardson Bay to San Francisco Bay proper, and construction began on 21 buildings, six shipways, two outfitting docks and thousands of feet of track for movable cranes. The Administration Building, begun on April 25, was ready for occupancy on June 17. The 122,000-square-foot warehouse, largest structure in the yard, was begun on May 2 and completed on July 28. The second-largest building, the 107,000-square-foot Mold Loft, was completed on August 23.[8]

Even while the yard was under construction, shipbuilding got under way. Marinship laid its first keel on June 27, less than four months after Admiral Land's initial telegram. The first ship was launched in September, just six months after the signing of the Commission contract. By the end of 1942, construction of the facility was essentially finished.

Marinship then employed 19,000 workers and had already delivered five ships. In less than ten months, Pine Hill and its adjacent waterfront of marshes and tidelands had been transformed into the largest industrial

Marinship under construction, 1942. Blasting the hillside to make way for the yard.

installation ever built in Marin county, before or since.

During its three-and-a-half-year career, Marinship delivered 93 vessels: 15 Liberty Ships and 78 T-2 tankers (including a few that were modified as Navy oilers). The yard also outfitted and repaired an additional 23 vessels and began building barges for the invasion of Japan, a project that ended abruptly when Japan surrendered. Marinship delivered its last vessel in October 1945, and shortly thereafter all major work ended. The yard was formally decommissioned at midnight, May 16, 1946.[9]

Marinship was thus a military-industrial comet, briefly lighting up the Bay Area economic skyline. The yard was smaller and less publicized than Henry Kaiser's great Richmond complex, but Marinship was in many ways the most technologically innovative and efficient of all the Bay Area's shipbuilding plants. At Marin, the application of mass production techniques to ship construction (Eliot Janeway called it "a reasonable facsimile of line production") may have reached its highest stage of development.[10]

The yard's story, however, is more than just an account of technological innovation and production miracles. Marinship was important in the development of Bechtel, today one of the nation's most powerful corporate empires. The yard was an example of the cooperation between government bureaucrats and corporate managers that evolved during the New Deal and World War II eras, a cooperation between the public and private sectors that still characterizes much of the nation's defense economy. In the workplace, Marinship had to cope with new patterns of labor, gender and ethnic relations. The yard even spawned construction of a vast housing project that planners hoped to mold into a particularly enlightened working class community. Ultimately, the story of Marinship is one of extraordinary social change and economic accomplishment framed and motivated by wartime conditions. Frances Jackson and her neighbors were just the first of tens of thousands of people whose lives were dramatically affected by the coming of World War II to Pine Hill.

CHAPTER TWO

Joint Venture

IN 1921, THE CONSTRUCTION companies owned by W. A. "Dad" Bechtel and Henry J. Kaiser were each working on projects near Redding, at the northern end of California's Sacramento Valley. Kaiser decided to visit the Bechtel site and the two future building magnates met for the first time. It proved a fateful encounter for both men. Their two companies became entwined in a number of joint business ventures that were to change the face of the American West and, in the process, eventually lead to the Bechtel management of Marinship.[1]

Dad Bechtel had left his family's Oklahoma farm in 1898 to work in railroad construction. By the turn of the century, he had located in California and in 1906 started his own construction firm. He initially installed his family in a comfortable home on Oakland's Adams Point, later moving to larger and more rural surroundings in San Leandro, a few miles south. By the 1920s the company had moved into highway construction, taking advantage of increasing state and local contracts for paved roads resulting from California's spectacular automobile boom.

By this time, Henry Kaiser had also moved to the Bay Area after engaging in various business ventures in other parts of the United States and Canada. He opened a sand and gravel quarry near Livermore, about 30 miles southeast of Oakland, and, like Bechtel, entered the lucrative road building business. By the late twenties, Kaiser and Bechtel already had been involved in several joint projects, sometimes combining with other western construction companies, including Morrison-Knudsen of Boise and Utah Construction of Salt Lake City. Joint ventures became increasingly common as the size of projects grew, reflecting the enormous expansion of the western economy. Individual companies had neither the capital nor experience to bid on complex contracts and so banded together in various temporary combinations.

As business expanded, Dad Bechtel expanded the scope and structure of his enterprise. In 1920, he was instrumental in founding what became the Industrial Indemnity Company, an insurance firm providing workers' compensation coverage for California building companies. In 1925, Bechtel formed his first corporation, the W. A. Bechtel Company, with headquarters in San Francisco. By now the senior Bechtel had brought his three sons, Warren Jr., Stephen and Kenneth, into the business, and the "boys" soon took seats on the corporation's board of directors. 1925 was also the year the company began its first water project, a dam on Bowman Lake in the Sierra Nevada.[2]

In 1931, Bechtel and Kaiser were instrumental in forming a consortium of companies to bid on the nation's largest pending public works contract, the federal Bureau of Reclamation's proposed high dam on the Colorado River. Initially, some of the member firms planned to bid against each other, but at a meeting at the Engineers Club in San Francisco in February 1931, just two weeks before bids were due, they banded together to submit a joint proposal. Eight companies were involved in the effort, but at the suggestion of Felix Kahn of MacDonald and Kahn, the consortium whimsically adopted the name "Six Companies Inc." after the informal title of San Francisco's association of Chinese benevolent societies. The Six Companies construction combine won the Boulder Dam contract with a low bid of $49 million and completed the project two years ahead of schedule. The massive, highly publicized effort catapulted Bechtel, Kaiser, and their associates into the ranks of major national construction firms and put them on the track of other lucrative public contracts, including projects emanating from the vast New Deal public works program. It also reinforced the strategy of large-scale joint ventures that Bechtel, Kaiser, and their partners were to continue for more than a decade.[3]

Dad Bechtel was the original president of the Six Companies, but he died unexpectedly in 1933 while on a trip to the Soviet Union. Within the family firm, Steve, the middle son, became the dominant figure, also serving on the four-man Six Companies executive committee, chaired by

Henry Kaiser. In 1937, Steve established an important link between Bechtel and John McCone, a Southern California businessman and former college classmate at Berkeley. The new Bechtel-McCone Company, headquartered in Los Angeles, specialized in constructing chemical factories and oil refineries, including the Standard of California plant in Richmond and the Union Oil refinery at Oleum. Bechtel-McCone also eventually won lucrative foreign contracts in countries such as Venezuela and Saudi Arabia.

At the same time, Bechtel participated in major new ventures with all or some of its Six Companies partners. The consortium established a procedure whereby one firm would serve as sponsor of a project, taking major administrative and financial responsibility but inviting other partners to participate for smaller shares of the work and profits. In this form, Bechtel joined in building such major public works as Bonneville Dam on the Columbia River, Parker Dam on the Colorado River, the San Francisco-Oakland Bay Bridge, and the original Broadway (or Caldecott) "Low Level" Tunnel through the Oakland-Berkeley Hills. After 1939, the companies increasingly followed federal dollars into military projects, Bechtel taking major responsibility for construction of the Oakland Army Base and Fort Ord on the Monterey Peninsula.[4]

The establishment of the United States Maritime Commission in 1937 and its policy of underwriting the growth of the U.S. Merchant Marine precipitated the Six Companies entrance into shipbuilding. Steve Bechtel discussed the new federal program with his East Bay neighbor, Earl Fisher, vice president of Pacific Gas and Electric Company, and an appointee to the Maritime Commission. Bechtel also explored the matter with Six Companies participants Charlie Shea and Henry Kaiser, who in turn contacted influential friends in Washington, D.C. and the Pacific Northwest. The result was a 1939 joint venture between the Six Companies and Todd Shipyards of New York to build five Maritime Commission cargo vessels in the Seattle-Tacoma area. In 1940, through Commission intervention, the Six Companies-Todd combination contracted to build 30 cargo ships for the British government at a new San Francisco Bay facility in Richmond. Todd soon withdrew from the Richmond venture, and the Six Companies, with Kaiser as dominant sponsor, established sole control of the rapidly expanding complex. This was the beginning of Henry Kaiser's vast wartime industrial empire, spanning both coasts but concentrated in Richmond, California, and

Portland, Oregon. Either as chief sponsor of Six Companies yards or as owner of his own plants, Kaiser was the nation's leading World War II shipbuilder.[5]

The British ships built at Richmond, with some design alterations, became prototypes of the American mass-produced Liberty Ships. In 1941, the Maritime Commission gave Richmond its first Liberty contracts and encouraged the Six Companies to develop additional West Coast yards to build more of what President Roosevelt called the "ugly ducklings." One result was the Calship yard at Wilmington, near the Los Angeles harbor. Bechtel was the project's chief sponsor, with Steve Bechtel serving as chairman of the board, John McCone as president, and Kenneth Bechtel as vice president. According to Bechtel company historian Robert Ingram, the rest of the board of directors "looked like a Six Companies reunion," including Les Corey of Utah Construction, Gilbert Shea of J. F. Shea, Henry Morrison of Morrison-Knudsen, Felix Kahn of MacDonald and Kahn, and Henry Kaiser and his son Edgar. At the height of operations, Calship employed more than 40,000 workers. In four-and-a-half years the yard completed 467 vessels. The combined output of Calship and Marinship made Bechtel the Maritime Commission's third largest wartime producer, after Kaiser and Bethlehem Steel.[6]

Bechtel also participated in another important Six Companies enterprise related to shipbuilding. In 1941, the consortium gained control of the Joshua Hendy Iron Works in Sunnyvale, on the Peninsula south of San Francisco. The historic company, which previously had specialized in mining and milling equipment, was put to work building reciprocating engines for Liberty Ships. Within two years, the firm's labor force expanded from 60 to over 11,500. Steve and Kenneth Bechtel were on the Joshua Hendy Board of Directors with a familiar cast of Six Companies characters, including John McCone, who served for a time as company president. During the war, Joshua Hendy produced about a third of all the Liberty Ship reciprocating engines, as well as turning out turbine power units for other types of vessels.[7]

Even before the United States formally entered World War II, the Six Companies enterprises had established an impressive ship construction record. Unlike more experienced shipbuilding firms, Kaiser, Bechtel, and their associates had few preconceptions about marine construction methods and technologies. The newcomers were able to innovate and adapt the revolutionary prefabrication and assembly-line techniques necessary to produce ships in unprecedented quantities and with unprecedented speed. Having little experience with skilled shipyard workers, the companies made effective use of inexperienced laborers. The new managements were unscarred by the industry's previous labor conflicts, and, as only temporary producers, were not afraid to establish new precedents in labor relations. As construction firms, they could build as well as operate the shipyards and were accustomed to short-term projects with rapid start-ups. Finally, they were supremely confident enterprises, growing with the West Coast economy and possessed with vast experience in obtaining federal dollars and turning them into productive facilities and healthy profits. Speaking of Henry Kaiser's entrance into the Maritime Commission's shipbuilding program, Eliot Janeway somewhat tartly observed that "it was a sand-and-gravel contractor's dream come true—at cost-plus."[8]

Given the partners' record of accomplishment, it is not surprising that on March 2, 1942, the Maritime Commission turned to the Six Companies participants, asking them to bid on a contract for another West Coast shipyard. As we have seen, Bechtel responded immediately and was chosen to build and operate the new yard. Within the company, Kenneth Bechtel had major responsibility for the new enterprise. Thirty-eight years old at the time of Marinship's founding, Kenneth was the youngest of Dad Bechtel's boys. Like his brothers, Kenneth had attended East Bay public schools and the University of California at Berkeley. During vacations he and his brothers had worked on company construction projects, beginning as laborers and gradually taking on more responsibility. In 1925, the boys became members of the firm's board of directors.

The Bechtel company history described Kenneth as a "financial man and administrative head," perhaps implying a personality very different from that of either his self-made father or his take-charge brother Steve.[9] In 1931, as Steve took increasing responsibility for the firm's construction activity, Kenneth became president of Industrial Indemnity, the company's insurance enterprise. Although he was involved in many other Bechtel projects, Kenneth also found time to develop a deep interest in yachting, the Boy Scout movement, and natural history and conservation.[10] A former Marinship executive described him as a "withdrawn, private person . . . . Completely unlike his brother Steve." There was something about Kenneth that "didn't allow him to be happy. [He] didn't get personally close to people," yet "he handled people well, was

Marinship in full operation. Administration Building is in upper right foreground. Below it are storage yards, covered prefabrication and preassembly areas, and four-story Mold Loft Building (still standing today). Shipways are in the center and outfitting docks and warehouse are at the far left. In the upper right background is the Marin City housing project.

sincere." Kenneth was so unassuming that when he walked
into the yard's temporary hiring hall in the spring of 1942, a new employee tried to recruit him as a blue collar worker. Bechtel demurred,
explaining that while he'd like to work, he didn't have a union card.[11]

Much of the rest of Marinship management had experience on previous Bechtel projects. General manager William Waste, the number two
man at the yard, had been administrative manager at Calship before
coming to Marin. Son of a former California supreme court chief justice,
Waste had grown up in Berkeley and met Steve Bechtel at the University
of California. During World War I, Waste briefly worked as a riveter in
an East Bay shipyard before serving in the Army. He finished his
education after the war and became a shipping executive. In 1931, Steve
Bechtel recruited his old college friend to serve as a manager on the
Boulder Dam project. Subsequently Waste worked on other Bechtel-Six
Companies ventures, including construction of the San Francisco-
Oakland Bay Bridge. In 1941, he was the first employee assigned to
Calship, and in March 1942 he became Marinship general manager even
before Kenneth Bechtel traveled to Washington to sign the Commission
contract. A former co-worker remembered Bill Waste as a decisive man
of strong, if not always rational, opinions. Once, when urged to give a
pay raise to a pipe-smoking employee, the general manager replied, "I
would never give a raise to anyone who smoked a pipe." Later he did in
fact grant the raise and after the war recruited the pipe-smoker to fill a
high-paid Bechtel position.[12]

Several other Bechtel veterans also obtained Marinship management
positions, including construction manager Ted Panton and chief engineer
Bruce Vernon. Still others had at least indirect ties with Bechtel or Calship. Administrative manager Robert Digges had worked on a Southern
California construction project near Calship and in that capacity had
come to the attention of John McCone. Assistant administrative manager
Jack Chambers was with the Los Angeles firm that handled Calship's
accounting. In 1942, his employers assigned Chambers to the new Marinship account, and in early 1943, he went to work for the yard itself.[13]

Marinship was initially administered as the "Marin Shipbuilding
Division of the W. A. Bechtel Company." In Six Companies tradition,
Bechtel had invited other firms into what in fact became a joint venture.
Included were sister company Bechtel-McCone, J. H. Pomeroy and
Company, Raymond Concrete Pile, and Six Companies veterans Mac-
Donald and Kahn, and Morrison-Knudsen. The lesser partners primarily

participated in the initial construction of the yard, but since the Maritime Commission only paid fees for production rather than construction, all shared in the enterprise's eventual profits.[14]

In the fall of 1942, Marinship became a separate corporation. Of the 4,500 shares of stock issued (with a nominal value of $100 per share), W. A. Bechtel Company and Bechtel-McCone each owned 1,375 shares, or one-third of the total. In addition, Kenneth Bechtel personally held 500 shares, giving the Bechtel group nearly three-fourths of all Marinship stock. The rest of the shares were apportioned to the remaining partners: 375 each to MacDonald and Kahn and Morrison-Knudsen, and 250 each to Raymond Pile and J. H. Pomeroy. The board of directors reflected the dominant Bechtel influence with Kenneth Bechtel serving as president and Steve Bechtel and John McCone as vice presidents. Other board members included B. M. Eubanks, Kenneth's and Steve's brother-in-law, and yard executives William Waste (who eventually became a vice president) and Robert Digges. Finally there were representatives of the partner companies, including those Six Companies perennials, Felix Kahn and Henry Morrison, who were in danger of spending all their time attending Six Companies-related board meetings.[15]

Conspicuous by his absence was Henry Kaiser. Marinship seems to have been the first Six Companies shipbuilding venture without Kaiser participation. Perhaps Kaiser and Bechtel were now so large that they did not need each other. Also by 1942, Henry Kaiser apparently regarded wartime shipbuilding as part of a permanent corporate shift of emphasis to industrial production. The Bechtel family, on the other hand, saw the wartime program as a temporary move away from the traditional focus on construction and engineering. Kaiser was also developing a considerable talent for self-promotion, while the Bechtels kept a comparatively low profile. Kaiser was hailed as a maker of production miracles, but with notoriety came resentment and controversy. He was criticized for taking too much credit, earning unfair profits and exercising undue political influence. Writing in 1960, former Maritime Commission chairman Emory Land contended that "thanks to good press relations," Kaiser "received credit that was not due to him." Land pointedly left Henry Kaiser off a list of "topflight ship production men," while including son Edgar Kaiser (and Steve Bechtel and John McCone).[16]

Perhaps, then, the Kaiser connection was becoming too bothersome and controversial for the Bechtels. By the end of the war, the two family companies had bought out each others' shares in Richmond and Calship, thus breaking the remaining major shipbuilding ties between them. Testifying at postwar congressional hearings on shipyard profits, Kenneth Bechtel and John McCone took pains to disassociate the Bechtel yards from the Kaiser operations. The relationship that had begun at an obscure construction camp near Redding two-and-a-half decades earlier was coming to an end, and with it, an important chapter in the economic development of the West.[17]

Marinship management. Stephen Bechtel is on far left, Kenneth Bechtel second from right, and William Waste on far right.

CHAPTER THREE

The Maritime Commission

ON NOVEMBER 23, 1943, KENNETH Bechtel wired Admiral Howard Vickery of the Maritime Commission that the tanker, the *Mission Purisima*, was completed, albeit behind schedule. "It's a girl," Bechtel explained. "Delivered at 6 p.m. November 23. Child is very healthy. All parents weak but will recover." Vickery replied with one of his typical "Vickery needles": "The delivery was stimulating news. But I hope the next period of gestation will not be that of an elephant."[1]

The acerbic tone aside, Vickery's message reflected the nature of the relationship between Marinship management and the Maritime Commission. Officially, the Commission owned the enterprise, but in fact it was the yard's only and anxious customer. What concerned the Commission was not Marinship's day-to-day operations or its profits and losses, but its output. The Commission needed ships produced and delivered as quickly as possible, and, in return, was willing to pay costs plus a reasonable profit. As Vickery put it, "What we were buying was management brains."[2]

The Maritime Commission was originally a peacetime New Deal agency, established by the Merchant Marine Act of 1936. By that year, more than 90 percent of large U.S. commercial ships were over 20 years old, many of them at or on the edge of obsolescence, thereby threatening the nation's commercial and military status. Thus, in addition to granting the Commission regulatory powers over the commercial shipping industry, Congress encouraged the production of new vessels by allowing the

Commission either to grant construction subsidies to private companies or to contract for new ships itself. Joseph P. Kennedy, father of the future president, was the first chairman of the new commission, but he soon resigned to take a more prestigious government position. President Roosevelt then appointed his old friend, Rear Admiral Emory S. Land, to the Commission chair.[3]

An Annapolis graduate who as a midshipman achieved distinction as both student and athlete, Land served in the Navy Bureau of Construction and Repair during Roosevelt's term as Secretary of the Navy from 1913 to 1921. In 1937 Land took early retirement to accept the president's appointment to the Commission. After ascending to the chairmanship, he assumed personal control over Merchant Marine policy, running the Commission as a centralized agency. After Pearl Harbor, Land's power increased, as the president also appointed him to head the War Shipping Administration. An old Washington hand, the admiral had influential contacts in both the executive and legislative branches of government. According to Frederic Lane, chief historian of the Commission's wartime program, Land was a tireless worker with "a flair for salty phrases." He was also an impressive witness before congressional committees, "where his footwork was just as agile as it had been on the football field."[4]

The heart of the Commission's production program was its Technical Division, headed by Commander (later Admiral) Howard Vickery. Like Land, Vickery was a product of the Navy's Construction and Repair Bureau. He initially served on the Commission staff, but became a full member in 1940 and eventually was appointed vice chairman. As Land became increasingly occupied with lobbying and broad policy matters, Vickery took virtually full responsibility for the construction program. He visited Marinship six times during its three-and-a-half years of operation, while Land made only one trip. Vickery worked at a pace "which awed and inspired his subordinates," but it also seems to have undermined his health. He suffered a serious heart attack in 1944, yet insisted on returning to work in less than four months. Vickery retired from the Commission at the end of 1945 and died in March of the following year.[5]

In 1939, the Commission announced its first construction program—a plan to produce 50 ships per year for ten years. The vessels were designed to be among the most sophisticated and efficient ships afloat. The C-class cargo ships, such as those built by the Six Companies-Todd combination in Seattle, for example, had carrying capacities of between 9,000 and 12,500 deadweight tons and, for their time, impressive top speeds of between 14 to 16.5 knots. Almost before it began, however, this long-range program was interrupted by the wartime emergency. In 1940, as German U-Boats took their toll of English shipping, the Roosevelt Administration assisted the British in finding American builders for 60 emergency freighters, 30 of which were manufactured at the Six Companies-Todd yard at Richmond. In addition, the President ordered the Maritime Commission to produce 200 American merchant vessels within a year, a goal he doubled to 400 in January 1941. Roosevelt was asking the Commission to build 80 percent of its ten-year goal in just one year.[6]

The Commission clearly could not build sophisticated C-class ships quickly enough to meet the emergency goals, so Vickery and his staff sought instead a simple vessel type that could be rapidly mass-produced. Several existing ship plans were considered, but eventually the Commission decided on a modified version of the British vessels being successfully built at Richmond and elsewhere. The ships' capacity of 10,419 deadweight tons was similar to that of the C-class vessels, but their designed speed of 10 to 11 knots was considerably slower. The new vessels were powered by old-fashioned reciprocating engines rather than modern turbines. The Commission formally designated the ships "EC2s," but the public relations staff soon dubbed them "the Liberty Squadron," or "Liberty Ships." During the war, American shipyards eventually produced over 2,700 Liberties. They constituted over half of the Commission's total wartime shipping program, measured in vessels or deadweight tonnage.[7]

The emergency program soon overwhelmed American's ship construction industry. In 1937, there had been just ten U.S. yards capable of building 10,000-ton cargo vessels. By 1941 that number had increased, but existing plants were occupied with a rapidly expanding naval construction effort. Thus, while the Commission continued to contract with private yards, it was also forced into the construction business, establishing its own yards, including Calship.[8] The West Coast, with a substantial amount of existing, untapped industrial potential, was most dramatically affected by the Commission program. From 1941 to 1945, West Coast yards received more than half of the total Commission contracts, while the East Coast's share was less than one-third. (The remainder went to Gulf and Great Lakes yards.) In contrast, the Navy's

military ship construction program, which was largely accomplished by
existing, old-line yards, was concentrated in the East. Well over half of
naval construction contracts went to East Coast yards, while the West
Coast's share was under 20 percent.[9]

In 1941 the Commission's program produced over one million
deadweight tons of shipping capacity, nearly tripling the 1939 figure.
Nevertheless, the total 1941 Merchant Marine output of both American
and British yards did not equal that year's losses to U-Boats. For 1942,
President Roosevelt announced an ambitious goal of five million tons,
raising it to eight million after the attack on Pearl Harbor. For 1943,
Roosevelt asked for an astounding 16 million tons, four million more
than the total capacity of the entire American merchant marine in
1941.[10] These figures produced a rapid expansion of existing
Commission facilities, and, in the spring of 1942, the Commission established the last six of its 21 yards. Included among the 1942 plants was
Marinship.[11]

Admiral Howard Vickery, U.S. Maritime Commission, flanked by William
Waste on the left and Kenneth Bechtel on the right.

The Maritime Commission also partially decentralized its operations in 1942, opening four regional offices around the country. The West Coast office in Oakland was by far the most important, for it supervised over half of the total Commission construction program. Carl W. Flesher, West Coast regional director of construction, was an Annapolis graduate who had worked for Westinghouse before joining the Commission staff. He reported directly to Admiral Vickery in Washington. Although Flesher had an excellent record, his fellow regional directors were sometimes targets of well-aimed "Vickery needles." In September 1942, for example, the admiral noted that the Great Lakes region had managed to produce only one ship. In a wire to the regional director, he inquired, "Do you desire a spur?"[12]

The Maritime Commission's presence at Marinship and other yards was limited to a few dozen staff members. They included a resident engineer, auditors, supply and material coordinators, a purchasing controller, an industrial relations specialist and various machinery and hull inspectors. Former Marinship executive Jack Chambers was "struck by how good those people were at their jobs," but the jobs had little to do with the actual operation of the yard.[13] Instead they assured that Commission performance standards were met and Commission funds were properly spent. Even then the federal personnel sometimes had difficulty exercising their authority. Historian Frederic Lane concluded that Commission staff members often had less experience and received far less salary than the private managers they were expected to regulate. But the Commission's weak presence at the yard was consistent with Admiral Vickery's operating philosophy: "We talk to management, but we do not go in and try to run their plant. You have to give management freedom . . . ."[14] In the case of Marinship, the freedom was so great that Commission personnel had not even visited the proposed Sausalito site when they signed the operating contract with Bechtel.[15]

Once the yards were operating, the Commission attempted to stimulate production by promoting athletic-like competition between the companies. The Commission staff established a series of awards, commemorated by banners and flags that winning yards were allowed to display. In January 1943, Marinship received an "M for Merit" banner for having achieved the greatest production of any of the new yards established in the spring of 1942.[16] In September 1943, the Commission announced a "Tanker Champ" flag, awarded to the yard with the greatest bimonthly tanker production. In addition to Marinship, Alabama

Shipbuilding, Bethlehem-Sparrows Point in Baltimore, Sun Shipbuilding of Pennsylvania, and Swan Island, a Kaiser facility in Portland, were in the competition.

All of the yards specialized in T-2 tankers, though Sun had the greatest experience with tanker construction. But the two West Coast plants, Marinship and Swan Island, eventually dominated the contest, regularly passing the Tanker Champ flag back and forth. In January 1945, Kenneth Bechtel and William Waste wired "Eddy" Kaiser announcing that they were sending the "weather-beaten" flag back to Portland. Marin had delivered ten ships the previous two months, while Swan Island had produced 13. "This flag has flown so long and changed hands so often," Bechtel and Waste pointed out, "suggest we jointly buy a new one. Better yet, when our boys win it back, suppose you send us a new one."[17] As the wire indicates, the yards took the competition seriously. When Marinship won its first Tanker Champ flag in the spring of 1944, the event was celebrated by a spontaneous parade of 5,000 workers.[18]

Far more important to the yard than awards were Commission supply requisitions. By the time Marinship began production, the Maritime Commission had established a centralized procurement system, whereby all major materials and supplies were purchased and distributed by the Washington office. In January 1943, the Commission concentrated purchasing for all yards in a new Procurement Division, while distribution was the responsibility of the Production Division.[19] This centralization made it inevitable that Marinship would establish a Washington office to deal directly with Commission personnel who controlled the supply pipeline. The yard's Washington staff included four executives and three secretaries. The office communicated with Sausalito primarily by teletype, and the two teletype operators, one in Washington and the other at the yard, became good friends, though they never met each other face to face or even spoke to each other by phone. In addition to filing formal procurement requests and meeting other procedural requirements, the Washington staff attempted to cut red tape and lobby on behalf of Marinship, which was competing for attention with approximately 70 other major Commission contractors.[20]

The Washington office also worked with Marinship's eastern subcontractors to assure timely delivery of components. In 1945, for example, a Washington staff member traveled to the New Jersey plant that was producing the main condenser for the tanker *Huntington Hills*.

Marinship's first vessel, the Liberty Ship *William Richardson*, underway on Richardson Bay.

The Marinship man worked for a day, helping the factory overcome difficulties it was having with the part. He then arranged for an Army cargo plane to deliver the condenser that evening to Hamilton Field, an air base a few miles from Sausalito. A truck hauled the 2,700-pound component to the yard outfitting dock where it was immediately installed. At 5:30 p.m. the next day, the *Huntington Hills* returned from its trial run, ready for delivery in a world record time of 33 days after keel laying.[21]

Sometimes the Washington staff was involved in less earthshaking activities. Marinship received Commission permission to name its Liberties after important people in California history, its first tankers after California missions, and its later ships after California oil fields. In 1945, the yard's management decided to call one of its ships the *Marin Hills* in tribute to the plant's home county. The Commission bureaucracy turned down the name on the grounds that oil had never been produced in Marin. The Washington office did some quick research and discovered that a producing exploratory well had been drilled on the Sausalito waterfront in 1904. With this documentation, the Commission reversed its decision, and the *Marin Hills* was duly launched.[22]

While Marinship's Washington staff tried to influence government officials and subcontractors, the Maritime Commission itself was lobbying furiously on behalf of its programs. In 1941, the War Production Board granted the Commission equal priority with the Army and Navy for scarce industrial supplies. After Pearl Harbor, however, the armed services were given higher status, and Admiral Land had to go directly to President Roosevelt to get the Commission's equal priority restored. Even after Roosevelt's decision, it took all of Land's considerable influence and Washington connections to keep Commission contractors adequately supplied.[23]

Early in the war, the most serious shortage was in steel. While American steel production grew by over 50 percent from 1939 to 1943, the increase still did not meet wartime demand. In 1939 shipbuilding used only 1.3 percent of the nation's steel; by 1943 the figure was over 20 percent, including 60 percent of all steel plate.[24] Competition between the Commission and Navy construction programs was particularly intense, with neither obtaining satisfactory amounts. Marinship was reduced to fabricating scrap steel from old bridges and railroads to build Liberties, while Kaiser received federal funds to construct California's first complete steel mill at Fontana.[25]

The steel shortage played a major role in the Maritime Commission's decision to shift Marinship from Liberty to tanker production in the fall of 1942. By that time, the Commission recognized that there was not enough available steel to maintain the rapid rate of increase in Liberty production. On the other hand, a shortage in tanker capacity was hampering the war effort. The Commission reasoned that shifting Marin's effort would reduce short-term demand for steel as the yard retooled and reorganized, while producing a much-needed long-term increase in the nation's tanker fleet.[26]

The steel shortage and the conflicts it created were not substantially alleviated until the end of 1943. By that time, in spite of the shortage, the Maritime Commission had achieved remarkable results. In 1942, the Commission accomplished the President's goal of eight million deadweight tons of new construction. The following year's goal of 16 million tons was actually exceeded by over three million. In 1943 alone, the Commission program produced nearly 50 percent more carrying capacity than had existed in the entire U.S. Merchant Marine in 1941. By the end of 1942, the amount of new tonnage built by allied yards was greater than that lost to German submarines. In effect, the Liberty Ship had defeated the U-Boat.[27]

The Maritime Commission's greatest influence over the yards was its power of the purse. While the Commission reimbursed companies such as Marinship for the actual costs of plant construction, profits were earned only on shipbuilding contracts. During World War I, the government contracts had paid all expenses, plus a set percentage of costs as profit. Critics charged these "cost-plus" agreements provided no incentive for rapid performance and encouraged contractors to spend heavily, since profits increased as costs grew. When the Liberty Ship program began in 1941, the Commission tried to avoid these problems by creating "cost-plus variable fee" contracts which reimbursed operators' expenses but provided fees or profits that were adjusted up or down depending on performance. Initially, yards were awarded a $110,000 fee per vessel for a "standard" performance of 500,000 man-hours per ship. If the yard bettered the standard, it could receive as much as $140,000; if performance was substandard, the fee could be as little as $60,000. As the average time to complete a Liberty dropped during 1942, the Commission adjusted the fee schedule accordingly, but the basic "cost-plus variable fee" principle remained. Similar in concept were "cost-minus" contracts which also awarded fees on the basis of performance.[28]

All of Marinship's initial Liberty and T-2 tanker contracts were either "cost-plus variable fee" or "cost-minus" agreements. On March 1, 1945, however, all future and pending contracts were changed to a "lump-sum" arrangement. These contracts paid a set fee per ship, but the yard was responsible for all costs. The Commission set the price for T-2 tankers at $2.8 million and allowed a maximum profit of $200,000 per vessel. The contracts required Marinship to take more risks, since costs were no longer guaranteed, but allowed the yard to earn higher profits. In fact, Marinship earned more than the $200,000 per ship maximum and eventually had to return over $2.5 million in excess profits. After the war, the yard was also required to absorb $644,000 in other "non-reimbursable expenses."[29]

In spite of Commission efforts to reduce "excessive" fees, critics often charged that contractors were guilty of gross profiteering. A Senate investigating committee led by Harry Truman found "rapacity, greed, fraud and negligence" on the part of some companies. The House Committee on the Merchant Marine and Fisheries held hearings on shipyard profits in 1944 but issued no report, apparently because it feared the conclusions might weaken the war effort.[30] Such concerns obviously vanished after the war, and in September 1946 the Committee again took up the issue.

The Committee had before it a report by Ralph E. Casey, an auditor for the General Accounting Office, that was highly critical of the Commission construction program. Casey condemned the concentration of Commission contracts in very few corporate hands, charging the major talent of such enterprises was "knowing how to secure a contract from the Maritime Commission." His most serious charge was that contractors had garnered huge profits in return for negligible investments. Since the commission owned the yards, paid all capital costs and purchased major equipment and supplies, the operators had spent almost no money and taken virtually no risk. The result was an extraordinary return on investments. Henry Kaiser, for example, had earned "something like 11,600 percent" on his original expenditure. Although Kaiser was the major focus of the report, Casey did not ignore the Bechtel operations. He calculated that Marinship received total fees or profits of $11,871,394 on Commission contracts of $280,941,573. In three-and-a-half years, Bechtel and its partners had earned a more than 2,000 percent return on their original investment of $500,000.[31]

In his testimony before the Committee, Kenneth Bechtel pointed out that in the case of Marinship, the Commission had solicited the Bechtel Company's participation rather than vice-versa. While he did not deny that the partners had only invested $500,000 in the venture, he claimed that the yard normally had operated with a short-term private debt of about $1 million to maintain cash flow between Commission reimbursements. Bechtel argued that this debt should be included in the stockholders' risk along with the original half-million dollar investment.[32] While he was technically correct, the risk resulting from the indebtedness was hardly serious. No one doubted that Commission payments would eventually cover the obligation.

Bechtel was on stronger ground when he observed that Casey's figure of $11 million-plus profits was *before* taxes. During the war, the federal government collected a surtax and an excess profit levy, in addition to normal corporate taxes. The result of this triple burden was that Marinship's *after*-tax profit was $3,862,734, just a little over one-third of the before-tax figure. but this does not completely vitiate Casey's point. The $3.8 million total still represents a return of more than 700 percent on original capital investment.[33]

Admiral Land argued that the issue of capital investment was irrelevant. Repeating Admiral Vickery's often-stated point, he told the Committee that the Commission had not contracted for investment, but "management brains."[34] Marinship's profits should thus be considered management fees, a payment for services, rather than a return on investment. The question, then, was whether after-tax profits of about $41,000 per ship were excessive. But "excessive" compared to what? Apparently that was a question the Committee was not prepared to answer, and in Marinship's case, no action resulted from Casey's charges.

Henry Kaiser, of all people, may have expressed the moral dilemma best. He contended that he supported any effective plan "to take the profit out of war." However, he claimed to know of no country "that won a war without an incentive to production," and in a capitalist economy, that incentive was profit. In her newspaper column, Eleanor Roosevelt agreed, pointing out that "Labor, too, was well-paid." The *New York Times* also reminded the Committee it was investigating "a success not a failure." Business may have profited greatly, even excessively, but, the *Times* exclaimed in its headline, "WE GOT THE SHIPS."[35]

T-2 tanker, *Mission Purisima*, on trials in San Francisco Bay.

CHAPTER FOUR

Line Production

"WE ARE NOT ONLY BUILDING ships," Admiral Land observed in 1942, "we are assembling ships. We are more nearly approximating the automobile industry than anything else."[1] Land's observation referred to the assembly line, mass-production manufacturing methods used by Marinship and other Maritime Commission yards. The twin foundations of the new process were prefabrication and preassembly. Of the 250,000 separate items that went into a Marinship vessel, most were already shaped and fitted together before the manufacturing process ever reached the shipway. Only a little over 100 separate units, some as large as an entire deckhouse, were actually assembled on the way, and another 200 items were added at the outfitting dock after launching.

Prefabrication and preassembly allowed employees to work on parts for several ships at the same time and, compared to traditional practice, tied up the shipway for a relatively short period. They also allowed management to break down the construction effort into more than 200 separate skills so that inexperienced workers could be trained in just one or two specialized jobs rather than the broad range of skills normally expected of a shipbuilder. Assembly line methods based on prefabrication and preassembly thus not only resulted in spectacular feats of production but also decisively shaped the social environment of Marinship's world of work.[2]

Some American shipyards had experimented with assembly line techniques as early as the 1890s. But the new methods were not widely adopted because there was little demand for rapid, large-volume production. World War I, however, produced such a demand, and several yards, including some on San Francisco Bay, built freighters by the assembly line process. Ironically, none of the emergency World War I merchant ships were completed before the conflict ended.[3] During the Second World War, the Maritime Commission attempted to avoid previous mistakes, and the Liberty Ship effort differed from the World War I program in several respects. For example, prefabrication for the Liberties took place at the shipyard rather than the steel mill, somewhat minimizing the delays in steel deliveries. The Liberties were almost entirely welded rather than riveted, again speeding the production process. Welding had the additional advantage of being easier to teach to inexperienced workers, especially if many of the welds occurred in the fairly comfortable environment of a preassembly area.[4]

The application of line production methods to the Liberty program had dramatic results. On the average, Commission yards produced their second round of Liberties in half the time of the first. The tenth round was finished in one-fifth the time and the thirtieth round in one-tenth the time of the first. In the fall of 1942, Kaiser's Oregon Ship Yard launched a Liberty Ship just ten days after keel laying. Richmond Yard No. 2, also a Kaiser operation, responded by assembling a launchable vessel in just four days. These were highly publicized efforts, produced largely for public and media consumption, but by 1943, several West Coast yards were regularly launching vessels after 20 days or less on the shipway. The total number of worker-hours expended per Liberty Ship, on or off the way, declined by one-half during the war years, with by far the greatest drop occurring in 1942, the year the ratio of ship tonnage built to tonnage sunk turned decisively in favor of the Allies.[5]

Because of its late arrival on the scene, Marinship was able to take advantage of the line production experience of the earlier Commission yards. Several Marin executives and key craftsmen had previously worked at Calship, and the Southern California yard prefabricated components for the first six Liberties produced at Marin. Most important, Marinship's physical layout reflected the experience of Calship and the other Commission yards.[6]

Marinship operated as a giant, mile-long, north-south assembly line. Steel plates arrived by rail or truck at the north end of the site, where the two-ton slabs were stored in vertical racks. In the Mold Loft Building, also in the northern portion of the yard, ship architects and engineers modified standard Commission plans and produced wooden models of

Marinship at work. Shipways with prefabricated parts in the foreground. Components are moved from the preassembly area on the left by giant overhead cranes.

the ships' major components, some more than 300 feet long. The steel moved south from the storage racks to the plate shop, where it was cut and shaped into parts on molds produced from the wooden models. Next, the parts moved further south to the subassembly area, where much of the actual putting together of the ship occurred. Finally, the preassembled components were transformed into a launchable vessel on one of the yard's six shipways, located just south of the subassembly area. Key to the whole process were giant, ten-ton capacity overhead cranes.[7] On a traditional assembly line, the line itself moved the product by conveyer belt through various stages to completion. In a shipyard, however, the components were far too large for the line to carry them. Instead, cranes transported major parts along a stationary production path to the point of launching.

The launchings themselves were major events at Marinship. The hoopla created by the ceremonies produced favorable publicity for the yard and, management hoped, improved employee morale. Before the first launching, that of the *William Richardson* in September 1942, Kenneth Bechtel told one of his secretaries, Daisy Edmonds, "we have ditch-diggers and dam-builders who've never launched ships, and we're finding out there's a lot of protocol .... Will you take care of that?"[8] Mrs. Edmonds in fact handled "protocol" for all 93 Marinship launchings. She made sure there was a woman sponsor for each ship. The sponsor, whose chief task was to swing an accurately-aimed bottle of champagne across the bow at the proper time, sometimes was a well-known Bay Area personality or wife of a prominent citizen. But sponsors also came from the ranks of the yard workers and their families. The wife of a Marinship carpenter won a lottery to become sponsor for the *Richardson* and eventually became something of a yard celebrity, attending the formal ceremonies and lunches that preceded each of the remaining 92 launchings.[9] Daisy Edmonds was careful always to have a "co-sponsor" on hand, in case the main champagne-swinger didn't appear. To assure that the ship would move down the way and into the water at the appointed time, jacks were strategically installed to give the vessel an extra boost.[10]

The actual launching was preceded by speeches and entertainment. Joseph James, a welder and accomplished singer who figured prominently in yard protests against racial discrimination, performed at several of the ceremonies. Sometimes the event was combined with a "Family Day" celebration, when Marinship opened its gates to friends and relatives of the workers. Such was the case on March 28, 1944 when thousands of spectators watched Mrs. W. B. Lardner launch the tanker *Mission Carmel*. Mrs. Lardner, whose husband and two sons also worked at Marinship, was chosen for the honor by her fellow employees in the Engineering Department. Chief engineer Bruce Vernon served as master of ceremonies, and the event included a performance by a mezzo soprano from the San Francisco Opera Company and a speech by Carl Flesher, regional director of the Maritime Commission. The mayor of Carmel and a Catholic priest from the Carmel Mission were also in attendance.[11]

In spite of their ceremonial significance, the launchings did not end work on the ships. After the speeches and champagne, the vessels moved to the outfitting docks at the south end of the yard. Here the last 20 percent of the work was completed, including installation of lifeboats,

weapons and other deck apparatus, finishing and furnishing the interior
cabins and galley, and stocking the ship with more than 50,000 separate
items, most of which were stored in the giant warehouse located near the
docks. Once the outfitting was completed, the ship took its trial run
through San Francisco Bay to the waters off the Farallon Islands, about
20 miles to the west. Representatives of the Maritime Commission, the
American Bureau of Shipping and the Coast Guard put the vessel
through a series of tests before approving formal delivery to the
Commission.[12]

In the spring of 1942, Captain Vickery asked Marinship to produce
Liberties "with all possible speed."[13] The company responded in spectacular fashion. Of the six Commission yards established soon after
Pearl Harbor, Marin was first to get under way. It launched its first vessel 51 days ahead of schedule and delivered the ship in just 126 days,
nearly half the average time taken by other new Commission yards.
While the Commission hoped that Marin would produce three Liberties
before the end of 1942, in fact the yard delivered five ships. Of course,
Marin received invaluable help from Calship during this crucial period;
nevertheless, production of five vessels, while the yard itself was under
construction and while an inexperienced work force was being recruited
and trained, was an impressive accomplishment.[14]

Even as Marinship celebrated its successful start-up in Liberty
production, the yard faced a new challenge: the shift to construction of
T-2 tankers.[15] The T-2s were originally planned as part of the
Commission's long-range program drawn up in the 1930s. They were
not simple ships designed for mass production like the Liberties, but
state-of-the-art vessels, as advanced as any of their class on the high
seas. As such they presented a far more formidable construction task
than the Liberties. For example, each tanker contained 16 miles of pipe
whose installation required 17,000 individual welds.[16] Marinship had to
double and redouble its pipe fabrication facilities to apply the principle
of preassembly to the T-2s.

The tankers were also far less standardized than the Liberties. Sun
Shipbuilding of Chester, Pennsylvania was already producing T-2s with
6,600 horsepower engines, but Marin initially was to build ships with
10,000 horsepower drives. The first Marinship tankers were for fleet use
and had to meet Navy as well as Maritime Commission standards. Over
the next three years, the yard turned out tankers for both the Maritime
Commission and the Navy, some with 10,000 horsepower engines and

A sponsor breaks champagne across the bow at a Marinship launching.

U. S. MARITIME COMMISSION TANKER

S. S. ESCAMBIA

FIRST TANKER SHIP LAUNCHED BY
MARINSHIP CORPORATION
SAUSALITO, CALIFORNIA

Keel laid on December 7, 1942   Launched on April 25, 1943
Total time from keel laying to launching: 139 days

SPONSOR   MATRON OF HONOR
MRS. JOSEPH COOPER   MRS. J. D. VARGAS
Wife of Marinship shipfitter   Wife of Marinship welder foreman

LAUNCHING PROGRAM

5:10 P.M. SUNDAY, APRIL 25, 1943

"Tankers Away" . . . . . JOSEPH JAMES, Marinship welder, accompanied by ALBERTA MAYO
(Words and music written for this occasion by Francisca Vallejo McGettigan)

Raising of the Flag . . . . . BOY SCOUTS OF TROOP 6, San Anselmo, under direction of Scoutmaster Clifford Romer

"The Star-Spangled Banner" . Led by MR. JAMES

Invocation . . . . RABBI ELLIOT M. BURSTEIN, Congregation Beth Israel, San Francisco

Welcome . . . . AL GRACEY, Superintendent of Hull Division

Remarks . . . . LAWSON LINDE, Hull Construction Engineer

Introduction of Matron of Honor and Sponsor . . . . MR. GRACEY

Response . . . . MRS. JOSEPH COOPER, Sponsor

Launching procedure . . . . . Explained by DON LIND, Hull Superintendent, Way 6

Launching of the S. S. ESCAMBIA, 5:30 P.M.

•

FIRST TANKER LAUNCHING AT MARINSHIP

Today's launching is dedicated to the men and women of Marinship, and to their families. Honor of designating their wives as Sponsor and Matron of Honor was given to two Marinship employees who were chosen as representatives of the yard by a selection committee. The committee, and the names of twenty persons from whom the two were designated, were drawn by Mrs. Anne Snead from a box containing the names of all Marinship employees. Selection Committee was composed of H. E. Waldorf, P. J. Donbrook, D. G. Skinner, and H. L. Wolhautter.

ESCAMBIA RIVER . . . According to U. S. Navy tradition, all tankers are named for Indian rivers. The Escambia rises in southeastern Alabama and flows through western Florida into the Gulf of Mexico.

Program, first tanker ship launching, April 25, 1943. The ship was built for Navy use and thus received a traditional Naval rather than USMC name. *(From the collection of Harlan Kessel.)*

others with 6,600 or 8,250 horsepower motors. A few of the Marinship T-2s were even modified to serve as Navy oilers. In each case, the design was somewhat different and the advantage of repeating exactly the same plan again and again was lost.[17] Finally, Marinship was expected to shift to tanker production while completing its last ten Liberties and finishing the construction of the yard and the initial recruitment and training of its work force. Under these conditions, the successful application of assembly line production techniques to the T-2s was the yard's greatest achievement.

It certainly wasn't easy. After a triumphant 1942, 1943 was difficult and disappointing. While the completion of the Liberty program went well, the start-up of T-2 construction was fraught with problems. Production manager R. L. Hamilton observed that the shift to tankers "all but knocked our mass education program in a cocked hat."[18] The first tanker was delivered behind schedule in 205 days, and, rather than improving with experience, the yard took 248 days to deliver the next T-2. During 1943 as a whole, Marinship managed to complete only 11 tankers, about half as many as expected. In July, Vickery told yard workers that he was pleased with the quality of their work, "but I'm never content with output." "You are on probation now," the recently promoted admiral warned, and "there'll be no room for alibis."[19]

Kenneth Bechtel did not make many alibis in his year-end report in the company magazine *The Marin-er*. He admitted that "we have fallen short of our original expectation on tankers." "We might as well frankly recognize," Bechtel conceded, "that the job of converting this yard to tanker construction and getting geared up on tanker deliveries was tougher and took longer than expected." But Marinship needed to shape up quickly, for the Maritime Commission expected the yard to deliver nearly 40 T-2s in 1944. "There will be a job for everyone who will work and take an interest in his work," the company president promised, but, "There will be no job for loafers." General manager Bill Waste warned that "Work or Else" would be the policy for 1944.[20]

These stern statements implied that the workers were primarily responsible for the problems in initial tanker production, but poor, inexperienced management also played a major role. As the shift to T-2s began, the yard embarked on what production manager Hamilton admitted was a "desperate experiment." Most Commission plants stock-piled subassembled parts: Kaiser, for example, tried to keep a backlog of components for 12 to 20 ships available at all times. But at the end of

1942, Marinship decided to go to a "straight-line" production system that eliminated nearly all stock-piling. The theory was to speed production by keeping the sub-assembled units on a tight schedule, moving parts quickly to the shipways. Some Bethlehem yards had experimented with such a system, but never to the extent that Marinship now planned.[21]

Straight-line production seemed to be a logical extension of the assembly line method and eventually proved worthwhile. But it depended on expert planning and execution to route needed parts and materials to the right place at precisely the right time. Initially, Marinship management was not up to the task. A breakdown in one part of the production process brought virtually the entire yard to a halt. According to Hamilton, morale suffered and "nerves were frazzled by the tension." "Coercion, policing, and cajoling" brought few results, and it is probably no accident that Marinship's most serious labor-management and black-white conflicts occurred during the difficult shift to straight-line tanker production. For most of 1943, yards using more traditional techniques, such as Sun Shipbuilding or Kaiser's Swan Island, were turning out tankers faster than Marinship.[22]

Not until the end of the year did Marinship's rate of production match that of its most efficient rivals. By then, the yard had gained needed experience in straight-line production, and management had made changes in the schedule and distribution of work. The yard, for example, had begun operations with three eight-hour shifts, seven days a week. But this meant that maintenance and repair of facilities inevitably interfered with production. In the spring of 1943, Marinship shifted to a six-day work week, with Sunday reserved for maintenance, repair and only emergency production. Changes were also made in the method of shift transfer. Originally all work stopped during transfer periods, but in 1943 management instituted a ten-minute overlap, allowing production to continue and the new shift to be briefed on work-in-progress.[23]

Most important, the company also instituted major improvements on the outfitting docks, where 20 percent of the work occurred. For much of 1943, all attention was devoted to reducing production time spent on the shipway, but by the end of the year outfitting had become a major bottleneck. Marinship was launching vessels far faster than it was delivering them. In December 1943, management decided to increase the size and quality of the outfitting crews. Production manager Hamilton described taking "every available man from the shops, from the skids,

Launching the Liberty Ship *S.S. Philip Kearney*, 1943.

and from the ways who had proved his ability as a team worker . . . and moving him to the docks." The strategy was successful, and "in a matter of days the outfitting bottleneck was broken."[24]

The results were dramatic. In January 1944, the yard delivered three new tankers; in February, two more; and in March, an additional four vessels. The March total established Marinship as the nation's bimonthly "Tanker Champ" for the first time, and for the rest of the war, the yard regularly vied with Swan Island for the honor.[25]

By early 1944, then, Marinship had proved it could build T-2s as fast as any Commission yard. But Swan Island and Sun Shipbuilding were still producing tankers for less money. Now that the immediate shortage of vessels had been overcome, the Commission was showing increasing concern about costs. It explored new contract arrangements that would require operating companies to absorb all or part of the expense of production.[26] Marinship managers thus began searching for new ways to increase the yard's efficiency. The result was the final major innovation, in many respects the last great extension of Marinship's line production process.

The company organized "flying squads" of specialists highly trained in a particular part of the assembly process. The squads, specializing in, say, hull or bulkhead assembly, moved from shipway to shipway, practicing their specialized craft. The innovation not only increased production speed, but also brought a steady decline in needed workers. As Hamilton described it, "Division by division, section by section, crew by crew, throughout the yard the streamlining continued. . . . All unnecessary jobs were cut. All inefficient workers were terminated."[27] Perhaps the production manager overstated the case a bit, but costs and the size of the work force did come steadily down. By the late summer of 1944, Marinship was not only as fast as any other tanker yard but also as cost efficient.

In 1944 the yard delivered a tanker on the average of every ten days. Hull 27, completed in January of that year, took 1,575,000 worker-hours to produce. Hull 66, delivered a year later, took just 736,000 worker-hours, a reduction of more than 50 percent.[28] By the time Marinship shifted to "fixed price" contracts in early 1945, the yard was well-prepared to absorb the costs of production. The company ultimately made greater profits on the fixed-price contracts than on the old "cost-plus-variable-fee" and "cost-minus" agreements that guaranteed production expenses. In April 1945, Marinship delivered the *Ellwood Hills* in a world-record tanker-building time of 59 days. Two months later the yard cut its own record nearly in half, producing the *Huntington Hills* in just 33 days—28 days on the shipway and five days at the outfitting dock. The *Huntington Hills* was delivered in one-sixth the number of days and one-third the number of worker-hours as the yard's first T-2 tanker.[29]

After the war, production manager Hamilton observed that none of the vessels built by Marinship suffered major structural or mechanical failure. "Never so much as a bulkhead leak!" he boasted. But Hamilton was prouder still of Marinship's assembly line manufacturing system. In spite of the initial difficulties, he believed that straight-line production "was ultimately the margin by which we surpassed all competitors. . . . It allowed us to streamline our organization at all times in keeping with the maximum efficiency of our assembly line." Hamilton also recognized that the yard's production process had human as well as material implications. "It provided the incentive for thousands of unskilled men and women to produce to the limit of their capacity" and "compelled teamwork which we found impossible to compel by any other means."[30] Marinship's assembly line, with its components of prefabrication and preassembly, straight-line production and flying squad organization, was an exercise in social as well as mechanical engineering. The Bechtel management team sought, and to a significant degree achieved, effective control and management of both people and machines.

CHAPTER FIVE

Workers and Management

IN 1942, GRANT PERKINS, A 17-YEAR-old from nearby San Anselmo, joined his mother as a worker at Marinship. He worked first in the Plate Shop and later as a ship wright and truck driver. More than 40 years after the fact, Perkins remembered his Marinship experience with something less than enthusiasm. There was "an awful lot of goofing off," he claimed. "It seemed like anybody that could get out of work did."

Mary Entwhistle Poole, on the other hand, was stimulated by her career as a Marinship welder: "It became so fascinating I *couldn't* leave." A schoolteacher in the small town of Galt near Sacramento, Mary applied for a job at the yard after her brother, a Navy sailor, wrote her "we need more ships." Her family was shocked when she gave up a respectable teaching position, but Mary remembered her Marinship work as "a wonderful job."[1]

Moses Beard came to the yard from Denver in 1942. He fondly remembered his hyperactive social life in Marin City, playing poker every Saturday night and performing in a jazz band. During the weekends, he recalled, "about all that we did was go to parties." Celia Grinner came to Marinship from Louisiana and couldn't get used to the Bay Area's steep hills, fog and winter rain. She was homesick and "cried for a month."[2] Like most Marinship workers, Walter Brown, a former San Francisco claims adjuster, was attracted by the high wages. A shipwright, he also made box lunches that he sold to his co-workers for 25 cents. Soon he was making "an absolute fortune."[3]

These varied recollections, taken from oral histories conducted in the mid-1980s, clearly indicate that there was no "typical" Marinship worker and no "typical" Marinship work experience. The yard's history was too brief and its labor force too diverse for a stable working environment and working class culture to form. Employees came and went with remarkable frequency. The maximum number of people employed at any one time never exceeded 22,000, but Marinship hired more than 75,000 workers during its brief three-and-a-half-year existence.[4] By necessity, recruitment and training continued for almost the entire history of the yard. Shipyard labor, once one of the most exclusive and skilled of blue collar trades, was now open to all--regardless of race, gender or previous experience. The work force, like the production process, was in a constant state of flux, a fact that affected every aspect of labor-management relations at Marinship.

The yard's experience in this regard was hardly unique. Between the beginning of 1941 and the middle of 1943, total U.S. shipyard employment increased by nearly ten times, and this in the midst of an unprecedented national economic and military mobilization. The shortage of workers was so acute that at one point Admiral Land called for an involuntary labor draft, but objections by unions and civil liberty groups defeated the proposal. Instead, each yard was left to recruit as best it could, assisted by the U.S. Employment Service.[5]

Marinship, at a disadvantage because of its late start, concentrated its initial recruitment efforts in San Francisco and the northern Bay Area counties. By the summer of 1942, however, the campaign encompassed virtually all of California. Yard representatives traveled throughout the state, contacting local employment offices, and speaking before service clubs, chambers of commerce and on high school and college campuses. A recruitment session at San Jose State College, for example, drew a crowd of more than 1,200 people. In late 1942, recruiters also began moving out of state, concentrating on the Midwest, South and Southwest, areas that traditionally sent migrants to California and that had good rail connections with the Bay Area.

Guy MacVicar, one of the first recruiters in the Midwest, doubted that he could persuade Minnesotans to move to Marin, but his doubts vanished when he told "the very first applicant" that the yard was located "just across the Golden Gate Bridge from San Francisco." "The light that shone in his eyes," recalled MacVicar, "showed us the magic California holds for so many." Henceforth, the yard always used the phrase "just across the Golden Gate Bridge" in its recruitment campaigns.[6] By mid-1944, Marinship employees came from every state in the union. About one-third of the work force had arrived in California during the previous 24 months, with Texas, Minnesota, Oklahoma, Missouri and Iowa sending the largest contingents. Louisiana, Colorado and Arkansas also made sizable contributions.[7]

The most dramatic recruiting efforts naturally occurred during the initial buildup in 1942 and early 1943, but the yard's labor agents could never relax. Marinship faced a particularly difficult worker shortage in the summer of 1944, when the yard received new contracts that produced a need for an additional 2,000 employees. More than ten million men and women were now in the military, and Northern California alone faced a deficit of more than 70,000 workers. The yard redoubled its recruiting efforts in the Midwest and South, and for the first time, the Maritime Commission allowed Marin to pay transportation costs of prospective out-of-state workers.[8] The August 5 edition of the company magazine, *The Marin-er*, was turned into a recruitment brochure, its cover proclaiming "MARINSHIP NEEDS YOU." Inside the editors assured readers that the yard "offers more than a mere job . . . it offers a new experience in living—creative work for war and peace, in America's most modern shipyard." The magazine emphasized that Marinship was located in "beautiful California," and included scenic photographs of nearby attractions, including San Francisco and, of course, the Golden Gate Bridge.[9]

One cause of the yard's ongoing recruitment problems was that a Marinship executive described as the "vicious practice" of worker movement from shipyard to shipyard. In the Bay Area, workers often shopped around, looking for better jobs and working conditions. Although the federal War Manpower Commission attempted to control the situation, "shopping around" continued in labor-short regions like the Bay Area. While Marinship supervisors condemned the practice in theory, they were more than willing to hire trained workers from other yards.[10]

Marinship often managed to maintain an adequate work force only by adopting extraordinary means. Blue collar employees included unprecedented numbers of women and minorities and many very young and elderly workers. At one time, Marinship executives claimed that 60 percent of the San Francisco Symphony was working at the yard. A four-hour "victory shift" was added for service personnel to work after their normal military duties. The crew of an Australian ship was put to work while their vessel was being repaired. Marinship even employed inmates from nearby San Quentin Prison, including a bank robber whose expertise with explosives was particularly useful during the yard's initial construction.[11]

Once recruited, workers reported to the hiring hall for processing. This involved a vast array of paperwork that, as far as many employees were concerned, made the procedure "worse than joining the Army."[12] Young men of draft age (18 to 38) had to produce their Selective Service cards. Since the government had defined ship building as an "essential industry," Marinship's Selective Service office could request renewable, six-month draft deferments for young men whose labor was deemed vital to the war effort. The yard made an initial request to the individual's local draft board, and, if that was denied, an appeal was forwarded to the state Selective Service office in Sacramento. Particularly in 1942 and 1943, the yard regularly requested large numbers of deferments. In the three months from the beginning of November 1943 to the end of January 1944, for example, Marinship filed 5,010 deferment requests, almost all of which were approved. As the demand for ships diminished in the spring of 1945, draft authorities toughened their standards, and according to yard general manager Bill Waste, it became "practically impossible to obtain deferments except for very specialized needs."[13]

With young men dying overseas, deferments were understandably controversial. One worker wrote *The Marin-er* that people considered him "a slacker." When hitchhiking, some drivers looked at him "with fiendish venom." The editors assured the young man that he was "an essential worker," not a draft dodger, and supported that assertion with statements from local military commanders. Nevertheless, the draft dodging charges continued. In April 1945, a laid-off worker complained that he had been fired while men with unnecessary deferments stayed on the job. *The Marin-er* answered that the yard "at no time has endeavored to retain any individual who was not absolutely needed," and claimed that deferment requests "were made impersonally on their merits according to due process."[14]

After workers had been recruited, hired, processed and deferred, they still had to be trained. Kenneth Bechtel noted that "better than 90 percent" of Marinship employees "had never worked in a shipyard before, and had never worked in the craft that they went to work in in our

Marinship's diverse, multi-ethnic construction crew posed on a completed superstructure.

yard."[15] In effect, Marinship and the other Maritime Commission yards were gigantic experiments in industrial education.

By the time Marinship began operations, the principle of breaking down shipyard crafts into small components and teaching those sub-crafts to inexperienced workers was already established, particularly in the Kaiser yards. In September 1942, the Maritime Commission formally adopted a set of training procedures and appointed a former education director at Kaiser Richmond as national director of training. Consistent with Admiral Vickery's beliefs in management prerogatives, however, each yard had great autonomy in devising its own educational program.[16] Marinship generally borrowed procedures already established at Calship and other Commission plants. In welding, by far the yard's largest craft, Marinship expected inexperienced workers to achieve "journeyman" status in 120 days or less. During that period, employees were classified as "trainees" and paid lower wages than their journeymen colleagues. Trainees spent about three weeks in the classroom, learning basic tack welding. Training also occurred on the job, or, as management called it, "learning by producing."

It was impossible to accommodate all classroom trainees in Marinship facilities, so the yard encouraged local high schools, adult education facilities and junior colleges to begin crash courses in welding and other shipyard trades. The company funneled federal funds to schools and colleges to pay for the new classes and in many cases provided the teachers. By late 1942, nearly 5,000 people were enrolled in such Marinship-sponsored classes in San Francisco and the North Bay counties. The yard also took advantage of similar classes sponsored by other defense plants.[17]

Marinship was able to handle the bulk of classroom instruction in its own facilities only after the first new hires were trained in 1942. Eventually, a major training center was built in the yard. As might be expected, the quality of instruction varied greatly. Electrician Les Walsh remembered an instructor "who couldn't put in a light above the sink." Mary Poole, on the other hand, recalled that although she was completely inept when she started welding school, her teacher kept encouraging her until she became highly competent. Poole said the experience taught her an invaluable lesson that she used in her postwar teaching career: "You can't give up on anybody. . . . Teach confidence."[18]

One of the most difficult problems was finding low-level supervisory personnel—leadermen, bosses of gangs of ten or 20 workers, and fore-

Instructor and women students at a Marinship training class.

men, supervisors of five or six leadermen gangs. The yard began operations with a few experienced craftsmen from Calship, but Marinship had
to generate leadership from its own ranks almost immediately. Management initiated brief supervisory classes and followed them up with more
advanced courses and discussion groups. Remarkable job mobility
ensued. Francis Doyle remembered that "if you knew how to weld, you
became a supervisor right away." Mary Poole had no previous welding
experience, but her leaderman refused to supervise an all-woman crew,
so Mary took the job before she had even achieved journeyman status.
Ed Vacha came to Marin after working at Richmond and as a result was
hired as a leaderman and quickly promoted to foreman. Within a few
months, he received another promotion, this time to general foreman and
superintendent. Sam Knoles had owned a sheet metal shop before the
war and soon was supervising 300 sheet metal workers at the yard.
Knoles was an exception in that he had previous experience. More

typical was the case of Walter Brown. A former claims adjuster, he found himself, at the age of 24, a leaderman shipwright with a crew of 20. Brown had to work hard and learn fast "just to keep ahead of the men and earn their respect."[19]

One of the first administrative divisions established at the yard was Employee Relations. According to R. W. Adams, the division manager, the goal was to "build a morale program." It sponsored talent shows and fishing derbies as well as baseball, basketball, bowling and boxing. Famous entertainers, including Bing Crosby and Marian Anderson, gave brief performances at the yard. The Employee Relations Division even put on a show of paintings by Marinship employees that was first displayed in the San Francisco Museum of Modern Art and then sent to the Soviet Union.

The division's most ambitious effort was the publication of *The Marin-er*. It was first issued in June 1942 as a monthly but soon began appearing twice a month in a 9 x 12 inch, three-color format. Initially edited by Marin County journalist Fred Drexler, the magazine contained news, exhortations and photo essays, presented in a popular, upbeat style. General manager Bill Waste contributed a regular column ("Straight From the Shoulder") apparently written by Waste himself in an informal, locker-room style. According to Adams, the publication was intended to be a "medium of self-expression and guidance." It tried to make the worker "feel important in his job."[20]

Almost as soon as it began, *The Marin-er* had competition. Workers in the Electrical Division joined together to produce what Adams called an "in-yard gossip sheet." In reality, it was an exercise in shipyard muckraking. Called *The Stinger* after a tool used to light welding torches, the publication was edited by yard employee John Connolly and did indeed have a sting, criticizing both management and workers. *The Stinger* initially was supported by worker contributions, but the Employee Relations Division, apparently considering the publication a healthy outlet for worker discontent, began "quietly" paying production costs. Management eventually decided, however, *The Stinger* had become "very destructive" to employee morale. Rather than quash the journal outright, the company merged it with *The Marin-er* and made Connolly editor of the joint publication.[21]

The result was a somewhat "stingless *Stinger*," according to the union newspaper *The American Labor Citizen*.[22] But the merger did not completely still Connolly's criticisms, at least when it came to commenting on employees' bad working habits. In the June 10, 1944 edition, he informed general manager Waste that "you ought to know that you can buy anything at Marinship on any shift, from an automobile to an insurance policy or second-hand crib." Connolly invited Waste to "drop around some evening and see the wise guys smashing light bulbs with rocks; lighting cigs and pipes with torches; throwing their dinner refuse in some guy's hat; burning their names and ruining steel." According to the editor, "there are some guys in the yard who would work for nothing just for the prowling privileges."[23]

Forty years after the fact, former Marinship employees confirmed the accuracy of some of Connolly's comments. Grant Perkins described "a bunch of guys trying to get the highest bucks and do as little as possible." Gerald Carlton recalled workers running lotteries, selling chances on houses and cars. Ed Vacha claimed that prostitutes worked the yard and that floating crap games and other forms of gambling were common. Although employees were not supposed to leave the yard during their shifts, Betsy Bronan remembered people sneaking over the fence to a nearby bar for drinks during working hours.[24]

But the oral histories also tell of dedicated workers, and even Connolly admitted that the malingerers were "decidedly in the minority." At least some of the goofing off seems to have been caused by poor management and production breakdowns that caused long periods of idleness. Grant Perkins and his fellow drivers spent much of their working time sleeping in their trucks because there was nothing else to do. Francis Doyle even attributed some of the gambling to the growing efficiency of the workers. As he and his fellow welders improved their skills, they began finishing jobs well before the shift ended and killed time playing cards and shooting craps.[25]

Another problem that bedeviled management was what *The Mariner* called "chronic absenteeism." The magazine reported that "a few repeaters," workers absent three or more days per month, were primarily responsible for the problem. During December 1943, 13.8 percent of the day shift (8 a.m.–4 p.m.), 14.1 percent of the swing shift (4 p.m.–midnight) and 25.9 percent of the graveyard shift (midnight–8 a.m.) fell into the "repeater" category.

Welders and burners (who cut and shaped steel components) had the highest "repeater" rates, and maintenance workers and warehousemen the lowest.[26] Not surprisingly, absentee rates were particularly high during cold and rainy months like December and during the swing and graveyard shifts. Nor is it surprising that the rates were high in difficult and sometimes dangerous jobs like welding and burning. Thelma McKinney remembered that welding in the double bottom of a tanker day after day was "like working in a dungeon." Leon Samuels recalled a heavy steel slab falling near him: "It mashed up my bucket and hat; I don't know how it missed me." Other workers described acetylene explosions and fires. Grant Perkins, who had to shape white-hot steel plates with a sledge hammer, remembered that "you worked until your pants caught fire or your hair singed."[27]

To prevent or treat injuries, Marinship had an extensive health and safety program. The yard had four first-aid stations and a small on-site hospital. The company also enforced a vast array of safety regulations and required employees to wear hard hats and other protective clothing. Mary Poole remembered that on warm days the heavy leather overalls that welders were required to wear made her sweat so much that she had to drink gallons of soft drinks and water to avoid dehydration. Despite all safety precautions, however, 24 Marinship employees died on the job.[28]

Neither workers nor management were aware of the most serious long-term health hazard of all. Marinship, like other World War II ship-yards, installed large amounts of asbestos for insulation, pipe coverings and other purposes. Ed Vacha remembered that "it was like it was snowing in the engine room" when asbestos insulation was being installed. A 1945 national study found almost no cases of asbestosis due to shipyard exposure and thus concluded that asbestos installation was not a hazardous occupation.

Unfortunately, the study's authors were unaware of the disease's 20-40-year incubation period. In 1978, the federal government estimated that 4.5 million shipyard workers had in fact been exposed to dangerous levels of asbestos since the beginning of World War II. By 1982, ex-posed workers and other citizens were filing more than 6,000 suits per year against Johns Manville and other asbestos product manufacturers, alleging that the companies had known of the long-term dangers since at least the 1930s. Gene Perry, a former Marinship painter, recalled that asbestos work was considered clean and desirable in the yard and that the asbestos installers were "very haughty," seldom associating with "messy painters" such as herself. Perry recognized the tragic irony of the fact that the installers turned out to have "the most dangerous jobs. . . . They didn't even wear masks."[29]

PLANT RUBBER & ASBESTOS WORKS

Asbestos workers. Workers and management were unaware of the long-term dangers of asbestos work, then considered a desirable job.

In theory, workers could take complaints about health and safety conditions to their union. All blue collar and some white collar employees at Marinship were covered by collective bargaining contracts. The yard dealt with a number of unions, including the Teamsters, Building Service Workers, Electrical Workers, Printing Specialists, Technical Engineers and Machinists. But the great bulk of yard workers were represented by the Metal Trades Department of the AFL, a consortium of unions led by the International Brotherhood of Boilermakers, which by itself had jurisdiction over a significant majority of Marinship blue collar employees.

The Boilermakers and their partners in the Metal Trades Department benefited tremendously from the war effort. Collective bargaining contracts had covered about 50 percent of shipyard workers in 1940, but the figure rose to over 90 percent by 1944. Although CIO unions had considerable strength in northeastern yards, AFL affiliates such as the

Boilermakers dominated the Pacific Coast despite a strong but ultimately unsuccessful CIO challenge in the Bay Area in 1941. As a result, the "bible" of collective bargaining relations at Marinship and other far western yards was the Master Agreement between Pacific Coast shipbuilders and the Metal Trades Department, its local Metal Trades Councils and affiliated AFL unions.[30]

The Master Agreement resulted from a federal government decision to standardize and stabilize shipyard wages and working conditions through uniform agreements applying to all employees and unions in each of the nation's major shipbuilding regions. The Pacific Coast agreement, signed in April 1941, was the first in the nation. The government was not technically a party to the contract between employers and unions, but federal agencies had a major role in enforcing the terms. For example, the Shipping Stabilization Committee, an agency of the War Production Board, adopted the agreement's provisions as the industry's legally enforced pay and working standards. Similarly, the Maritime Commission reimbursed contractors' labor costs according to the agreement's wage rates.[31]

For most of the war, the Master Agreement provided for a basic $1.20 per hour wage for journeymen laborers. Workers on the swing and graveyard shifts received a ten percent and 15 percent bonus respectively. Any work over 40 hours per week was paid time-and-a-half. Since Marinship's normal work week included both an extra eight-hour day and a ten-minute shift overlap per day paid on the overtime rate, journeymen on the day shift in 1944 earned about $270 per month. A graveyard shift journeyman who worked 54 hours a week (as some did during peak production periods) earned about $365 per month. These were very impressive wages for workers who had recently lived through the Depression.[32]

The Master Agreement also contained a "closed shop" clause, requiring employees to join the appropriate union before going to work at Marinship. In practice this meant that the yard hiring hall requested a union work clearance for each new hiree. The unions in the Metal Trades Department had thus used the national emergency to achieve one of labor's major collective bargaining goals, control of job access. In return, however, the unions agreed to a no-strike pledge for the duration of the war.

More importantly, the Boilermakers and their partners were forced to grant "journeyman" status to hundreds of thousands of new workers who had not gone through traditional apprenticeship programs. Prior to the wartime buildup, workers spent four years as apprentices before becoming journeymen. Now men and women achieved that exalted status after just three or four months. The "de-skilling" of shipyard work had thus profoundly affected the groups represented by the Metal Trades Department. In effect, fairly small unions of skilled, white, male craftsmen had been transformed into giant, ethnically and sexually diverse organizations of semiskilled, mass-production workers.

Employers, too, had to accept important changes in labor relations. Not only did the Master Agreement provide for relatively high wages and closed shop practices, but the Maritime Commission also ordered the establishment of Joint Labor-Management Committees at all yards with more than 1,000 employees. The committees only discussed ways of increasing production and efficiency and had little real power. But many employers still saw them as threats to management prerogatives, even an attempt to "sovietize" the shipbuilding industry. Old-line firms such as Bethlehem particularly resisted the wartime changes. To the extent that the new labor practices established postwar precedents, these companies had the most to lose. On the other hand, newcomers to the field, such as the Six Companies partners, had little to fear, since they were in the shipbuilding business only for the duration of the national emergency.[33]

The Six Companies combine had been militantly anti-union on its first job, the Boulder Dam project. But on subsequent federal contracts, it was forced to accept union workers and soon learned to operate peacefully and profitably with organized labor. Marinship's Bechtel management thus already had experience in cooperative relationships with unions. The yard established a high-level Labor Relations Committee and a Labor Counselor's office to deal formally with collective bargaining matters. But day-to-day problems were handled by labor coordinator John F. O'Connell and his staff.[34]

Thirty years old at the time of his appointment, O'Connell was a Richmond native who had worked as a boilermaker before becoming a teacher and counselor in the San Francisco schools. His selection as yard labor coordinator was approved by the AFL Bay Cities Metal Trades Council. O'Connell argued that his job was to assure that both labor *and* management followed the terms of the Master Agreement in a "fair and equitable manner." Driving around the yard in a red Chevrolet, he and his assistants dealt with immediate on-the-job disputes,

Boilermaker at work in the bowels of a Marinship vessel.

sometimes siding with workers rather than supervisors. As a result, O'Connell found that he could often rely on the cooperation of union leaders. When a worker in the Pipe Shop was chronically late and abusive to his boss, for example, O'Connell explained the problem to the union business agent who supported a management decision to fire the man. No wonder O'Connell believed that his "hands-on" method "proved indisputably the answer to the on-the-job labor relations problem."[35]

O'Connell's methods even helped deal with the few unauthorized work stoppages that occurred despite the union no-strike pledge. One of the largest such incidents took place on May 5, 1943, when both management and labor leaders were surprised by a walkout of about 300 workers. Initially, Kenneth Bechtel and Boilermaker local president Ed Medly denied the walkout had even occurred, but a *San Francisco Chronicle* writer witnessed and reported the event. The walkout may have been in part a reaction to the general tension and frustration caused by the yard's problems in shifting to tanker production. In addition, employees were upset over management's aggressive anti-absentee campaign. One worker claimed his supervisor threatened "if you're late once more, we'll turn your name into the draft board." Two days after the first walkout, workers held a sit-in to protest the demotion of a popular foreman. The dissidents denied they were unpatriotic in stopping crucial defense production: "we just can't do good work under conditions as they are here."[36]

Business agents Ed Rainbow of Boilermakers Local 6 and Rhue Brown of Boilermakers Local 9 initially backed the workers, calling on the Maritime Commission to investigate Marinship labor practices. The Metal Trades Council newspaper, *The American Labor Citizen,* said the walkout was caused by "managerial inefficiency" and "company instigated dissension." The *Citizen*'s anger increased when Sausalito police arrested vendors who were distributing the paper at the yard gates. But at a meeting of 800 workers, Rainbow and Brown urged employees to return to their jobs, citing the no-strike pledge and the war effort as arguments against the walkout. In a *Chronicle* interview, Rainbow said he would deal with the "troublemakers" who had caused the problem: "We have them pegged. Out they go." And so they went. As John O'Connell put it, "with the help of the business agents . . . we finally—by the elimination of a few men—cleared the problem up."[37]

One problem O'Connell was not able to "clear up" completely was jurisdictional disputes between unions. The breaking down of traditional crafts combined with inexperienced management often produced jurisdictional overlap and confusion. One night, after a dispute between shipwrights and shipfitters had halted production, O'Connell persuaded the business agents of the two unions to accept the status quo and let their national headquarters settle the long-term conflict. Not so easily resolved was a dispute between shipfitters and boilermakers, each represented by a different local of the Boilermakers union. Even a trip to union headquarters in Kansas City by O'Connell and other Marinship executives failed to resolve the issue, though, according to the Labor Coordinator, "the going was a lot smoother after that."[38]

The unions also complained about the quality of Marinship's health care and workmen's compensation practices. Ed Rainbow particularly criticized the company's insurer, the Associated Indemnities Company, for its refusal to pay compensation in certain cases. *The American*

Labor Citizen pointed out that the company was largely owned by
Bechtel and raised the possibility of a conflict of interest. After the
unions called for an investigation by the state Industrial Accident
Commission, however, the newspaper reported that the company
"showed much more concern and care."[39]

Perhaps the longest-lasting labor-management dispute involved the
food served at the yard. Marinship, like an army, moved on its stomach,
and like soldiers, Marinship workers complained constantly about the
quality of yard food. One employee urged that "everyone connected
with the yard canteens" be imprisoned in a tanker double bottom. "For
sustenance, they'd be allowed their own 'delicacies' and for companion-
ship, yard efficiency experts."

The only foods available for purchase by blue collar workers were
cold box lunches, beverages and snacks at stand-up counters around the
yard. Marinship's cafeteria, which served hot food, was located at the
north end of the site, convenient only for headquarters office workers.
The yard's top executives got free meals in a private dining room, a
practice hardly calculated to bolster worker-management solidarity.
Union complaints about the situation prompted a congressional investigation and, after months of study, a plan for a new 2,500-seat dining
hall. Unfortunately, the facility was never built, though the yard did
begin serving hot meals at new stand-up canteens in November 1944.[40]

In spite of the union activity on these and other matters, the role of
organized labor is a subject largely missing from most Marinship oral
histories. Unions do not seem to have been an important part of most
workers' lives. Joining a union was just another prerequisite for
employment, union dues just another deduction from the paycheck. The
situation at Marin was probably similar to that described by Katherine
Archibald, who worked at the Moore shipyard in Oakland. She noted
"the antagonism, indifference and ignorance" of most (though by no
means all) workers regarding organized labor.[41]

Archibald also criticized "the reluctance of the trade unions to
encourage real participation" by the new workers. She pointed out that
only about 100 people regularly attended meetings of her 17,000-
member local and most of them were old-time, prewar unionists "trying
to protect their status." Of course, shipyard union leaders realized that
virtually all the semi-skilled wartime "journeymen" would lose their
jobs and thus leave the union once the national emergency ended. While
this attitude was understandable, it was also short-sighted. During World

War II, the American trade union movement had a chance to engage and win the allegiance of millions of new workers. When they left the defense plants, these workers might have taken positive, pro-union feelings with them. As a Steamfitters union official admitted, "the unions missed the bus, they completely missed the bus."[42]

Years later, Marinship workers who remembered their time at the yard most favorably identified neither with management nor organized labor but with the job itself. "The best job I ever had," recalled Mary Poole. And for some, the job involved a profound feeling of accomplishment. After a launching, Ed Vacha noted, "You looked at a ship and said 'I had something to do with that.' " For some of the workers, the very diversity and inexperience of the labor force enhanced the sense of achievement. Walter Brown explained that "we didn't know what all we were doing when we started. I think that was one of the things that made it such a wonderful experience.... It was exciting, just going to work every day."[43]

Women and Men

IN 1942, 53-YEAR-OLD VIANNE Cochran, whose husband also worked at the yard, became Marinship's first female bicycle messenger. More than 40 years later, she remembered that "all the men and the young fellows that were in the yard resented every job that women had because a man had previously had it." Once, while making her rounds, a man "coughed and spat a big gob on my cheek." Cochran "wheeled around, followed him back to the plate shop, threw the bike down and made a running leap." Before she could do any damage, a security guard restrained her, so she took her grievance to the top, pedaling to the administration building and confronting Kenneth Bechtel himself. The yard's ultimate boss poured her a cup of coffee, heard her story and assured her that he "would take care of it." And so he did; by the time Cochran returned to the mail room, the spitter had been fired. She recalled that word of the incident quickly got around the yard: "Don't monkey with Jim Cochran's wife, 'cause if you do, you'll get a pink slip."[1]

Cochran's story illustrates much about the status of women at Marinship. Certainly it shows the resentment that male workers often displayed and the effective determination of many strong women to counter that resentment. But even in her victory, Vianne was known as "Jim Cochran's wife." (One suspects that Jim was seldom identified as "Vianne Cochran's husband.") More importantly, the story illustrates management's strong commitment to protect its women workers. Kenneth Bechtel's action may well have been prompted by a personal

Vianne Cochran, Marinship's first female bicycle messenger.

concern for Vianne Cochran's dignity, but his response also reflected the yard's dependence on female labor. Marinship needed to keep its women workers happy and on the job. As one executive noted, given the drastic labor shortage, "America's wartime achievements in shipbuilding could not have been realized without women workers."[2]

Of all the social changes in shipyard work produced by the war and the new methods of mass production and craft breakdown, none was more dramatic than the presence of large numbers of female workers. Shipbuilding traditionally had been an almost exclusively male occupation. At the beginning of 1940, there were only 36 female shipyard production workers in the United States. One East Coast firm claimed that no woman had set foot in its yard since the company's founding in

1869.[3] The war rapidly changed all that. By 1943, 160,000 women production workers were employed in American shipyards. The Far West, with its especially severe labor shortage and innovative managements, led the way. While Pacific Coast firms employed 36 percent of all shipyard labor by the end of 1944, they were responsible for 55 percent of the nation's female shipbuilders.[4]

The growing presence of women in the shipyards was part of a larger, overall expansion of America's female labor force. During the war, the number of women workers grew by six million, an increase of fifty percent. The proportion of women in the labor force increased from 27 percent to 37 percent, a greater expansion in four years than had occurred in the previous four decades. Again the trend was especially noticeable on the West Coast, with the number of working women in San Francisco nearly doubling during the war.[5]

Married women were a particularly important source of new workers for the nation. The high unemployment levels of the Depression years had reinforced traditional attitudes against working wives who were thought to take scarce jobs away from male breadwinners. At one point federal authorities actually fired female civil servants whose husbands also worked for the government. But the wartime emergency brought about a drastic transformation in public policy. "Rosie the Riveter" campaigns sought to change public opinion and attract married women into the work force. The proportion of working wives grew from 13.9 percent in 1940 to 25 percent in 1945. By the end of the war, nearly half of all married women under 45 years of age were working.[6]

Although the increase in the female work force during the war years was impressive, at least one-half of the women defense workers had been in the labor market before the war began. For these women, the national emergency provided a chance to leave service and domestic jobs traditionally reserved for females and take relatively high-paying industrial positions normally held by men. While appeals to patriotism certainly attracted some women into defense work, the promise of high pay was the primary motivation for most. Defense plant wages were about 40 percent higher than those for traditional women's jobs. Not surprisingly, then, half the San Francisco women who were already employed in 1941 shifted to defense work during the war years. Nationally, while women occupied only 8 percent of durable goods production jobs in 1939, they held 25 percent of such jobs in 1943.[7]

From the very beginning of its existence, Marinship hired women in traditional female job categories. Mary Skarzinski, a clerk in the hiring hall, may well have been the yard's first official employee.[8] She was the forerunner of hundreds of additional female office workers. Large numbers of women were also hired in the yard's cafeteria and canteens as cooks, sandwich makers and counter personnel. In addition, Marin employed women laborers to do routine cleaning and maintenance chores around the yard.

The big breakthrough came in the summer of 1942 when Marinship began employing women craft workers. Welder Dorothy Gimblett, a mother of three, was the first. According to Marcia Patterson, Marinship's women's counselor, Gimblett's initial appearance in her welder's leathers was a major event: "Production slowed down; men turned from their tasks in astonishment." Some male workers laughed and whistled, but, according to Patterson, Dorothy "strode on and set the pace for thousands of women who followed."[9] By the beginning of November 1942, Marinship had more than 500 female employees. Kenneth Bechtel called them "first-rate workers." Eighty percent were between 22 and 35 years old, 54 percent were married, and about half had children. Eighty-four percent were high school graduates, and, like their colleagues nationwide, more than 60 percent had been previously employed, the great majority earning less than $100 per month in their pre-Marinship jobs.[10]

The presence of new female production workers brought many changes to the yard. Adequate restrooms and locker facilities for women had to be built, and some of the new workers insisted that the yard obey state labor laws that required a ten-minute rest period every two hours for women employees. One yard executive believed that women who demanded enforcement of the law "took full and more advantage" of it, but labor coordinator John O'Connell admitted there was "some right on both sides" of the issue.[11]

O'Connell claimed "the problem of women" caused "confusion and misunderstanding and got a lot of publicity." After the war, he recalled that when the yard asked the Boilermakers union for clearance to hire the first six female welders, business agent Ed Rainbow refused. The organization's constitution made no provision for female members, and Rainbow referred the issue to union headquarters in Kansas City. In the meantime, the incident created "considerable unfavorable publicity" for the Boilermakers. One of the prospective workers insisted on her right to employment and, according to O'Connell, was "very impolite and

abrupt with Mr. Rainbow." Eventually, Kansas City gave its blessing
and the women went to work. The woman who had given Rainbow a
hard time became a union shop steward and, O'Connell said, "did a
commendable job." Business agent Rainbow was understandably
relived that the controversy was over; he claimed "he'd rather get hit
with a baseball bat than become embroiled with a bunch of women who
wanted to go to work."[12]

George Keeney, Marinship's employment manager, was another yard
executive who would "never forget" the decision to hire women
production workers. "That was really a problem," he remembered,
"But the results were good." Keeney instituted "special shipyard-
adaptability tests" to eliminate "patriotic but obviously unsuitable"
applicants. Individuals were required to carry a 25-pound bucket of
scrap metal around the hiring hall and climb up and down stepladders.
Apparently the tests were given only to women.[13]

The Employment Department's most important action in response to
the new female workers was to create a position of women's counselor.
Marcia Patterson, who held the position for most of the war, helped both
women and men adjust to the new labor environment. Patterson realized
the magnitude of the change she was expected to promote. She believed
it was far simpler to have the two sexes work side by side on a traditional assembly line than in a shipyard. In the yard, "women were doing
what was conceded to be a man's job. . . . Here was a woman with a
welding stinger in her hand, a burning torch or a heavy wrench." To
ease the transition, Patterson personally addressed every leaderman and
foreman training class, discussing women's attitudes, expectations,
competencies and possible physical limits. She also cited some successful historical examples of women in industry. Patterson also made a
point of talking several times to each group of female recruits, spelling
out what was expected of them, the problems they were likely to face
and some of the mental and physical adjustments they would have to
make.[14]

One of her subjects was the strict dress code for women production
workers. Patterson told the recruits that "clothing must be appropriate
for shipyard wear and the particular job to be done." That meant a
bandana or cap covering hair, no sweaters except under jackets, no open-
toe shoes, slippers or sneakers, no jewelry and long fingernails, and no
"excessive makeup."[15] Working at Moore shipyard in Oakland,
Katherine Archibald noted such rules were based "as much on princi-

Women welders in their "leathers." The hoods, heavy jackets and overalls were required apparel for welders.

ples of concealment and sexless propriety as on the purported aims of safety." *The Marin-er* made no bones about that fact, as far as Marinship was concerned. It reported that Patterson had "lowered the boom on allure.... In a word, sexless." But undoubtedly some Marinship workers, like some at Moore, "skirted the bare fringes of managements's dress codes" and engaged in what Archibald called "excited roving among droves of draft-exempt men."

Marin yard superintendent Albert Webb reported that "some women always had men hanging around them ... to flirt with." Webb apparently did not think to blame the men, as well as the women, for this supposed transgression.[16]

Women production workers were initially concentrated in welding. This was by far the yard's largest craft and thus had the greatest need for labor. In addition, yard managers believed women were suitable for welding because, in comparison with many other shipyard jobs, the craft did not require brute strength (though both men and women sometimes had difficulty dragging the heavy electrical lead wires around the yard). For many months, women welders worked only in the shops and sub-assembly areas where the work was not so difficult and conditions were relatively safe. But in May 1943, a "model crew" of female welders was assigned to the shipways, doing dangerous and difficult work on scaffolds and in hull interiors. The experiment was a complete success and by the end of 1943 women were working in all parts of the yard and in virtually every craft.[17]

In December of that year, Marinship employed 4,023 women, 23.3 percent of the total work force. There were 3,071 production workers, including 1,201 welders (40 percent of all workers in the craft), 352 boilermakers, 255 burners, 226 laborers and more than 1,000 others in various additional crafts. Another 952 women worked in non-production jobs, primarily doing clerical and food service work. Although pay in these positions was lower than in the crafts, workers avoided the physical exertion, noise, dirt and danger of the yard. In addition, the dress code did not apply. Josephine Doyle, a clerk in the painting department, remembered that "we dressed like a lady" while craft workers "wore overalls." Cafeteria employee Grace Pastori recalled that the women who worked with her were generally middle-aged. Young women tended to take production jobs "because of the pay."[18]

Women production workers seem to have performed their tasks about as well as men. Although women trainees took slightly longer than men to become certified welders (235 hours of training versus 221 hours), Kelly Thorton, a former secretary, established the yard record on the welding certification test. Marinship supervisors reported that men generally executed orders "with more understanding," but women worked more carefully and uniformly. Women had more accidents per capita, but men's accidents tended to be more serious. [19] Male managers sometimes resorted to stereotypes to explain the female achievements in the crafts. A Marin executive believed women made good welders because welding did "not require a mechanical mind." Another Maritime Commission yard manager argued that women had a talent for welding because the principle of the craft was similar to that of sewing.[20]

The greatest disparities between men and women workers were found in absentee and turnover rates. Women had far higher incidences of both, a fact that Marcia Patterson attributed to the dual role of worker and homemaker played by many female employees. As an unmarried welder in a Portland yard put it, "I'm glad I didn't have to come back tonight to a husband and four kids waiting for me to cook dinner. I'm glad I didn't have to do the family laundry. In fact, Jingle, Jangle, Jingle—thank God I'm single!" When married Marinship worker Eloise Gravis was asked how she spent her "spare time," she answered "doing the laundry and cleaning house."[21]

Women with children had a particularly tough time, especially if they were single mothers or their husbands were serving in the armed forces. Although Congress appropriated money for child care facilities, the program met only ten percent of the need. Even when child care centers were available, many mothers refused to send their children to the facilities. One Portland yard worker said "I don't want my kids playing with just anybody's kids."[22] Unlike Kaiser's Richmond yards, Marinship did not establish its own center, although the nearby Marin City housing project had facilities for preschool children. Marinship mothers often farmed kids out to friends of relatives. Some women worked evening shifts so they could be with their children during daytime hours. Gene Perry remembered that she did not worry about her school-aged children staying home alone. Sausalito had a "friendly, small-town" atmosphere: "In those days we didn't have to lock our doors." [23]

Women at Marinship and other Maritime Commission yards received pay equal to men within specific job categories. But women had far less chance of being promoted. Other than Marcia Patterson, Marinship had no female executives and very few female supervisors. Some yard managers believed that men would not take orders from women, but Patterson noted that in the two cases in which mixed crews worked under women leadermen, they "did splendidly." Moreover, Patterson claimed that female supervisors were able to "get much more work out of their all-women crews." Nevertheless, the yard had just 27 female leadermen and only one woman foreman. Even so, Marinship's record was better than most. The yard's Kay Davis, a former clothing store buyer, was in fact the only female shipyard foreman in the nation.[24]

If Marinship did not promote women very often, it did try to maintain their loyalty and enthusiasm in less tangible ways. In October 1944, for example, the yard held what it called "the world's first all-woman launching." Marcia Patterson served as mistress of ceremonies, a female worker was chosen as sponsor, and women dignitaries gave the

Marinship women's counselor with female workers.

customary speeches. Even the color guard was composed of military
nurses.[25]

Marinship management also used *The Marin-er* to bolster the morale of women employees and promote their acceptance by men. On
September 16, 1942, the magazine published an interview with welder
Eve Bryan Borelli, who admitted that she had heard negative comments
from some of her male co-workers. But for the most part, men had been
"wonderfully good sports about the invasion of their he-man's world."
Borelli believed that if women wanted to do "a man's work," they
should not expect "special courtesies." She did, however, appreciate
men "who respect a woman though she may be wearing overalls and
heavy shoes, and have a dirty face."[26] On February 2, 1943 *The Marin-er* featured another upbeat article, this time on Gladys Griffin,
"welder, wife and mother." The magazine used Griffin as an example
of a good worker who also successfully fulfilled traditional female roles

and duties. She was described as "pretty, hazel-eyed and blonde." She lived in a pleasant home with her two sons and her husband, also a Marinship employee. Although the article included some pictures of Griffin at work, most of the photos showed her home life, taking care of the children, doing domestic chores and dressing in fashionable clothes for an evening on the town.[27]

Three months later, on May 1, 1943, *The Marin-er* presented a somewhat different view of the female labor force. "Ask any woman worker at Marinship if she intends to go back to housekeeping," the magazine proclaimed, "and she'll tell you emphatically NO." *The Marin-er* celebrated the fact that shipyard labor was liberating women from traditional female occupations. One worker said she was "never going to feel satisfied to work in an office.... From now on I want to feel like I'm a producer in American industry." She did emphasize, however, that "when the war is over and the boys come home," women would be glad "to turn over our shipyard jobs to them."[28]

This last point, the alleged willingness of women to vacate industrial jobs "when the boys come home," was crucial. Marcia Patterson recognized that "many men still felt that women's place was in the home, but as long as the manpower shortage existed, the average man was reconciled to getting along with them on the job." In addition, there was a widely held conviction that after the war the economy would not produce enough jobs for all the ex-servicemen and the high unemployment of the 1930s would return. As a result, "women were all right in the crafts—for the duration only."[29]

A special women's issue of *The Marin-er*, published December 11, 1943, reflected these attitudes. It included Patterson's strong defense of women workers against criticisms made by what the magazine called "a flint-skinned old timer." But in direct contradiction to the major theme of its May 1 article, *The Marin-er* now quoted a number of women who claimed they were anxious to get back to more traditional pursuits. "It's fun," said one worker "but just as soon as possible I say let the men take over." Another looked forward "to work that is more suitable for a woman," while still another employee said she would be "glad to stay at home." One woman admitted, "I love my job and am glad it's helping to build ships for victory. But boy oh boy, I'll be perfectly happy to turn over my burning torch to a man and go back to keeping house for my husband."[30]

If various national polls taken during the war were correct, these women were in the definite minority. Over 75 percent of female defense workers polled by the federal government's Women's Bureau and the New York State Department of Labor indicated a desire to retain their current jobs or fill similar industrial positions after the emergency ended. Yet, as *Business Week* magazine noted, women were disproportionately affected by the "first mass layoffs" in 1945. One historian claims women were laid off at a 75 percent higher rate than men.[31] At Marinship, women made up 20 percent or more of the production work force from the fall of 1943 through the end of 1944. By July 1945, however, only 940 female craft workers remained out of a total production work force of 7,200. By August 31, Marinship employed only 538 women in the crafts.[32]

The defense industry layoffs thus produced a substantial drop in total female employment. Between 1945 and 1947, the number of working women in the U.S. declined from 19 million to slightly under 17 million, and the percentage of females in the total work force declined from 36 percent to 28 percent. Nevertheless, the 1947 total was still substantially higher than the 1940 figure. And after 1947, the number of female workers began to rise again; by 1950 it equaled the 1945 figure in gross numbers, though not in proportion of the work force. Moreover, in 1950 far higher percentages of married and middle-class women were employed than in 1940.[33]

In spite of these overall numerical gains, the employment gender gap reappeared in the postwar era. The bulk of jobs lost to women after the war were well-paying industrial positions. In California, for example, 145,000 women were working as production workers in October 1944; one year later, the figure was only 37,000. Women were increasingly forced back into low-paying service and clerical jobs. In 1946 the Women's Bureau found that 75 percent of former female war workers were still in the labor market, but the majority had suffered significant income declines. Seventy percent of jobs available for women by June 1946 paid less than 65 cents per hour, while only 40 percent of jobs available for men paid that little. The gap between male and female wages grew in the immediate postwar years until it exceeded even that of the late 1930s. In 1939 the average woman worker earned 62 percent of that earned by the average man; by 1950 the figure was 53 percent.[34]

As Marcia Patterson had foreseen, the great occupational gains made by women during the war were "for the duration only." In 1982, historian Susan M. Hartman concluded that the war's "most dramatic

impact" for women was the "withdrawal of men from their customary
positions . . . and the consequent need for women to undertake novel
activities." But the men returned and the sexually-segmented, dual labor
market of the prewar period reappeared. Nevertheless, Hartman believed
that the 1940s "laid the preconditions for an awakened womanhood in
the 1960s." She may have had in mind women like the Marinship
worker who planned to go "back to housekeeping" after the war. Even
though she was leaving industrial employment, she argued that the shipyard experience "made women confident. It has given us a sense of self-
security. . . . Because I have been able to engage in war work, I'll never
again feel helpless."[35]

Woman worker at Marinship.

CHAPTER SEVEN

Blacks and Whites

NATHAN I. HUGGINS, NOW A DIS-
tinguished historian, was one of
4,846 black residents of San
Francisco in 1940. He was in
junior high school and remembers
"how small a community we
were. . . . How self-satisfied everyone was, despite discrimination in
almost every line of employment,
pervasive restrictive covenants, and
powerlessness in city politics." Huggins also remembers "how ambiva-
lent everyone was about the wave of blacks from the South, brought to
man jobs in the war industries. The old [black] residents saw the new as
crude, rough and boisterous. They lacked the manners and sense of
decorum of San Francisco." But the newcomers made good wages and
formed what Huggins calls "the basis of black business in the city."
Blacks could no longer be ignored, and "complacency disappeared.
Racial tensions rose." Huggins notes that many of the old black
residents wished the newcomers "would all go back where they had
come from."[1] But they stayed and laid the foundations of most of the
black neighborhoods that still exist in communities surrounding San
Francisco Bay.

The great World War II migration is the most important event in the
history of black people in the Bay Area. The region became a new black
frontier, the African American population growing from less than 20,000
in 1940 to over 60,000 in 1945. The number of blacks in San Francisco
more than quadrupled during the war, while that of Richmond and
Vallejo grew by over ten times. Marin County's black population
increased several hundred fold during the war years. By 1945, blacks

had replaced Asians as the Bay Area's largest non-white minority and the chief target of prejudice and discrimination.[2]

The Bay Area migration was part of larger social and demographic movements affecting the nation's entire African American population. Wartime industries produced more than 600,000 new manufacturing jobs for blacks and attracted about one million black migrants from the rural South to the urban North and West. African American women were particularly affected, as total black female employment increased by more than a third during the war years. The proportion of black women working in agriculture was cut in half, and that engaged in domestic service declined from 60 to 45 percent. As one black woman defense worker in Southern California put it, "Hitler was the one that got us out of the kitchen."[3]

In the Bay Area, about 70 percent of the employed black newcomers worked in one industry—the shipyards. Blacks comprised less than three

Black workers made up more than ten percent of the labor force by 1944.

percent of the region's shipyard labor force in 1942, but that figure rose
to seven percent in the following year and to more than ten percent by
the end of the war.[4] In 1941, the Kaiser Richmond yards initially attempted to hire only whites in skilled trades, but protests from local
black leaders forced the company to reverse that policy. By the time
Marinship began hiring in the spring of 1942, blacks were being recruited at all Bay Area yards. The regional labor shortage was such that any
able-bodied man or woman, black or white, could get a shipyard job.
Marinship blacks, like white women, advanced rapidly to journeyman
status in welding and other trades but received few promotions to supervisory positions. Within particular job categories, workers received
equal pay and benefits, regardless of race.[5]

Blacks were by no means the only people of color hired at Marinship. In April 1942, Arthur Quong Juey became the yard's first Chinese
American employee, working as a laborer in the facilities department.
The cafeteria hired Chinese cooks, and in 1943 a few Asians also found
work as welders and clerical employees. The placement of even small
numbers of Chinese Americans in unionized, industrial jobs and in white
collar office positions was a major breakthrough, given the Bay Area's
long tradition of anti-Asian sentiment. The yard also hired Latino
employees, including El Salvadoran immigrants who were important in
the establishment of what was to become the Bay Area's large Central
American community.[6]

But blacks were by far Marinship's largest minority group, by mid-
1943 comprising nearly ten percent of all employees. The company
recruited black labor in states such as Louisiana, Texas, Arkansas and
Oklahoma that had convenient rail connections to the Bay Area. Leon
Samuels was attracted by a Marinship advertisement in his hometown
Shreveport, Louisiana newspaper. He contacted the yard recruiter on a
Thursday and was on the train to California by the following Sunday.[7]
Once hired, Samuels and the other black newcomers were subjected to
what management described as an "indoctrination program which
taught colored recruits who had never held a responsible job before, as
well as those from the so-called underprivileged portions of the country,
good work habits."[8]

Housing was a particularly difficult problem for the new black
arrivals. Public projects such as Marin City, located just north of the
Marinship yard, were open to black workers and their families, but the
projects accommodated only a small portion of the total labor force.

Most black newcomers were forced to compete for shelter in a private real estate market that was highly segregated. Many Bay Area neighborhoods had restrictive covenants attached to deeds that prohibited sale or rental of homes to minorities. Residents and real estate firms also practiced other less formal but equally effective tactics to keep neighborhoods and communities all-white. As a result, blacks unable to obtain public housing were crowded into those few areas that traditionally were open to minority residents.

No such neighborhoods existed in Marin County. Indeed, a Marin Housing Authority staff member believed that only one black family resided in the county before the war.[9] Most of Marinship's black workers commuted to the yard each day from San Francisco's Fillmore district. Before 1942, the Fillmore had a few hundred black families scattered throughout an essentially multi-ethnic working class neighborhood. Shortly after the attack on Pearl Harbor, however, President Roosevelt ordered all people of Japanese descent on the West Coast relocated into government camps. Several thousand residents of the Fillmore's Japantown had to leave their homes, opening up inexpensive housing in the neighborhood just as the influx of black workers began.

Even so, there was not enough space available. By 1943 about 9,000 African Americans were crowded into an area previously occupied by 5,000 Japanese Americans, and city health officials classified over 55 percent of black housing in the Fillmore as substandard. In 1945 the Fillmore was still a multi-ethnic neighborhood, but Lester Granger of the National Urban League warned it could become "another Harlem." Granger explained that San Franciscans were adopting "the social stereotypes of the East, and they want Negroes to stay in the Fillmore." A visiting congressman commented that "you people out here have to make a big decision—whether you want the Japs back or accept thousands of Negroes."[10]

Within the yard, black and white Marinship workers usually labored together peacefully and efficiently. Leon Samuels remembered "good relations between people." At Marinship he "met the best people I ever met." Another former black worker, Thelma McKinney, said that when she came to the yard, "there was no such thing as segregation." McKinney recalled that people were so busy "they didn't have time for racism." But she also remembered being refused service in a Sausalito cafe because of her race. Marinship management was well aware of such conditions. When black opera singer Marian Anderson performed at the yard, company officials were careful to take her to a restaurant they knew would serve blacks.[11]

A white Marinship employee later recalled "feeling terrible" about the racial prejudices of many of his fellow workers. Perhaps he experienced attitudes similar to those described by Katherine Archibald, who was employed at the Moore shipyard in Oakland. She believed most of her white co-workers shared a "race hatred that was basic." When she tried to explain to a woman from Oklahoma that prejudice against blacks was similar to the prevalent "anti-Okie" feeling, the woman accused Archibald of implying that Oklahomans were "no better than a nigger." Another worker responded to Archibald's plea for tolerance with the comment, "Well, a nigger may be as good as you are, but sure ain't as good as me." But Archibald noticed that whites rarely made such statements directly to blacks. A white welder explained, "If you call him that [nigger], he's liable as not to pick up a piece of pipe and break your head with it." According to Archibald, such fears usually kept an effective, if uneasy, racial peace at Bay Area shipyards.[12]

If Archibald was right about the prejudices of most, though not all, of her white co-workers, the chief shipyard union, the Boilermakers, accurately reflected the views of a majority of its members. The Boilermakers was a "lily-white" organization, excluding blacks from full membership. As we have seen, the union represented about 70 percent of the craft workers at Marinship and other Bay Area yards under the closed shop terms of the Pacific Coast Master Agreement.[13] Wartime conditions had given the Boilermakers control of job access, but the war had also created a multi-ethnic work force that threatened the long tradition of white-only membership. If the union enforced its membership restrictions, it could deprive the yards of thousands of needed workers and leave the Boilermakers open to charges of the very kind of undemocratic behavior against which America was supposed to be fighting.

The Boilermakers' racial policy was shared by many AFL craft unions. Some AFL affiliates, however, including the Shipyard Laborers union representing unskilled maintenance and construction workers at Marinship, had long championed nondiscriminatory membership policies. In the 1930s, the new CIO unions, particularly the West Coast Longshoremen, not only had black and Asian members, but also actively supported civil rights causes.[14]

Even the Boilermakers modified their racial policies in 1937. Prior to that, blacks had been totally banned from membership, but the union's

1937 constitution authorized the establishment of all-black "auxiliaries." As the term implies, the auxiliaries were not full union locals and their members did not have full membership rights. Instead, the new structures were subordinate to white locals, which controlled auxiliary policies and treasuries. Auxiliaries had no independent grievance procedures and could not hire their own business agents. Members had no vote on local union matters and no representation at national conventions. They also received smaller insurance benefits than white members.[15]

Bay Area Boilermaker locals avoided direct confrontations over the issue of auxiliary membership during the first year of the war simply by issuing clearances to black shipyard workers without requiring them to join the union or pay dues. But by February 1943, the black segment of the work force was too large to ignore. East Bay locals formed auxiliaries and required blacks to join and pay dues equal to whites as a condition of employment. The National Association for the Advancement of Colored People filed a complaint against this policy with the National Labor Relations Board, which criticized the auxiliary membership status but did not ban it outright.[16]

On the west side of the bay, Boilermakers Local 6, with jurisdiction over Marinship and yards in San Francisco, chartered Auxiliary A-41 on August 14, 1943. The local announced that henceforth black workers must join and pay dues to the auxiliary in order to receive their union work clearance.[17] The announcement provoked organized opposition by the San Francisco Committee Against Segregation and Discrimination, whose membership included several black Marinship workers. For the rest of the war, Marinship was to be a center of opposition to Boilermaker membership policies.

The Committee against Segregation and Discrimination was led by Marinship employee Joseph James. In his early thirties at the time of the dispute, James had grown up on the East Coast, studied music at Boston University and pursued a promising singing career in New York. He came to San Francisco in 1939 to appear in the all-black cast of the "Swing Mikado" at the Treasure Island Exposition and settled in the Fillmore when the fair closed. He was hired at Marinship in 1942, and in two months advanced from welder's helper to journeyman. By mid-1943, James was a member of one of the new "flying squads " of expert welders. He was also an active NAACP member and a recognized black spokesman at the yard. With all this, he still managed to keep up his

"Negro Advisory Board" for special 1943 *Marin-er* issue on black workers. Joseph James is seated with pencil in hand.

singing career and often performed at Marinship launching ceremonies.[18]

Just a week after the establishment of Auxiliary A-41, *The Marin-er* devoted much of its August 21, 1943 issue to a discussion of race relations at Marinship. The special issue was prepared with assistance of a Negro Advisory Board, headed by Joseph James. Management obviously was concerned about racial tensions, particularly following major race riots that summer in Detroit, Los Angeles and other American cities. James wrote the lead article, "Marinship Negroes Speak to Their Fellow Workers," calling on his readers to "turn our hatred, instead of against each other, against the forces of fascism." An editorial condemned discrimination and proclaimed that the war was being fought "to prove for all time the dignity and rights for individual man regardless of race, creed or color."[19]

Marinship soon found itself in the middle of a struggle to establish those very principles in the Boilermakers union. After three months, at least half of the approximately 1,100 blacks in jobs under Boilermaker jurisdiction still refused to join Auxiliary A-41. On Wednesday, November 24, 1943, citing the closed shop contract provisions, the union ordered Marinship management to fire 430 black workers unless they paid their auxiliary dues in 24 hours. The Boilermakers also warned an additional 150 workers they soon faced similar treatment.[20] About 350 people met in San Francisco that evening under the aegis of the Committee Against Segregation and Discrimination and voted unanimously to continue boycotting the auxiliary.[21]

On Friday, November 26, the company told about 30 blacks on the afternoon shift that they could not work because the union had withdrawn their work clearances. More workers were barred at the beginning of the graveyard shift that evening. Saturday morning, November 27, hundreds of black men and women gathered at Gate 3 to protest the layoffs. The protest soon grew to include about 800 workers and was described by the San Rafael *Daily Independent* as "Marin's greatest labor demonstration and most critical situation to arise since the San Francisco 'general strike' in the summer of 1934."

Sheriff's deputies and highway patrolmen arrived with nightsticks and tear gas "ready for any emergency." Two black deputies from Marin City assured the county sheriff they could keep order, and, reported the *Independent*, "they succeeded admirably." Joseph James and three other black workers, Preston Stallinger, Edward Anderson and Eugene Small, met with company officials and then addressed the crowd. James, Stallinger and Anderson urged those who still had union clearance to return to their jobs while continuing to boycott the auxiliary. But Small called on blacks "to stand pat and not return to work" until they had full union membership.[22]

How many workers took Small's advice is a matter of some dispute. The *San Francisco Examiner* reported that 1,500 walked off their jobs, but that figure is larger than the total number of Marinship blacks under Boilermaker jurisdiction. The *American Labor Citizen*, voice of the Bay Area Metal Trades Council, assured its readers that the trouble was caused by a handful of malcontents and that a "vast majority of Negro workers" remained on the job. More than 40 years later, Moses Beard remembered that most blacks joined the strike. "We walked out in protest and forced them to back down."[23]

Whatever the exact number of strikers, it concerned Admiral Land at

Maritime Commission headquarters in Washington. Initially, Land urged workers to join the auxiliary under protest, but when this plea failed, the admiral asked the company to suspend the layoffs. California Attorney General Robert Kenny made a similar request, pointing out that if ship production slowed, "more American boys are going to die, both white American boys and black American boys."[24] The company, however, insisted that under the collective bargaining agreement, it was obligated to bar workers without union clearance. Throughout the ensuing controversy, Marinship insisted it was simply an innocent bystander in a dispute between blacks and the union. By agreeing to dismiss the African American workers, however, the company accepted the legality of the union action. Management also eventually joined with the union in appealing court decisions that outlawed Jim Crow practices.

Ed Rainbow, the business agent of Local 6, argued that the closed shop agreement was recognized by the federal government and that blacks understood Boilermaker policy when they took shipyard jobs. Rainbow also claimed that Local 6 had no choice in the matter, since it was simply following national union policy.[25] That policy, however, had not prevented the certification of a few Chinese American workers, nor, for that matter, had it been enforced in the case of Rainbow himself, a Native American. For the Boilermakers, "white only" meant "no blacks."

By Sunday, November 28, 160 workers, including Joseph James, had lost their clearances. That evening about 1,000 people attended a committee meeting in a Fillmore district church where Eugene Small called for a boycott against organized labor. But James and other leaders argued that the fight was against segregation, not unions. Finally, the meeting decided to pursue legal action, and the next morning committee attorneys filed suit in federal district court on behalf of Joseph James and 17 other blacks. The suit asked reinstatement by Marinship and $115,000 damages from the Boilermakers. Judge Paul St. Sure issued a temporary restraining order, suspending the layoffs pending a formal hearing.[26] When the order was enforced on Friday, December 3, Joseph James announced, "Now we can get back to work." Committee sound trucks toured the Fillmore and Marin City, urging blacks to return to their jobs.[27]

In a formal hearing on December 12 in a San Francisco federal courtroom, Committee attorney George Anderson argued that if African Americans could be forced into separate auxiliaries, so could Native

One black woman war worker commented that it was Hitler "that got us out of the kitchen."

Americans like Ed Rainbow, Irish Americans (Judge Michael Roche) or Armenian Americans (defense attorney Charles Janigian). But the union refused to respond to this point, contending instead that federal courts had no jurisdiction in the matter. On January 6, 1944, the court agreed, granting the union's motion and dismissing the case.[28]

The dismissal automatically ended the restraining order, and Local 6 announced it would withdraw union clearance for workers who had not paid auxiliary dues by January 14. But on that day committee attorneys appeared before Marin County Superior Court Judge Edward Butler of San Rafael to argue the case on state rather than federal law. Judge Butler issued another restraining order prohibitng the layoffs. The order was served just 15 minutes before a work shift was about to change at Marinship, and the company already had removed black workers' time cards from the rack. But clerks hurriedly replaced the cards, and the shift changed without incident.[29]

While the case was being argued in court, the Boilermakers' auxiliary policy was investigated by the President's Fair Employment Practices Commission, established in the summer of 1941 in response to a threat by prominent blacks to stage a march on Washington to protest discrimination in defense and government employment. The march was called off only after President Roosevelt agreed to form a commission to monitor enforcement of non-discrimination policies in federal contracts and the civil service.[30] Although the FEPC had limited powers, it dealt a serious blow to the union cause on December 14, 1943 when it ordered the Boilermakers to "eliminate all membership practices which discriminate against workers because of race or color." The commission prohibited five employers, including Kaiser and Bechtel, from enforcing closed shop provisions that contributed to such discrimination. However, the employers appealed the decision, and the appeal procedures, necessitating new briefs and hearings, took a year to complete. In the meantime, the commission suspended its order.[31]

FEPC chairman Malcolm Ross hoped he could persuade the Boilermakers to change their membership policies in January 1944 at the union's international convention in Kansas City. This was also the intent of a resolution passed by East Bay Boilermakers Local 681. It requested the convention to allow full membership "without regard to race, color, creed, national origin or sex." Of 6,000 signatures gathered at Bay Area shipyards in support of the resolution, about 75 percent came from white workers.[32] Apparently, not all white shipbuilders conformed to Katherine Archibald's depiction of them as racists. The Kansas City convention received a similar appeal from 22 prominent black citizens. AFL president William Green criticized job discrimination in general terms from the convention floor, and delegates heard much the same from President Roosevelt via telegram.[33]

The convention, however, liberalized membership rules only to the extent that auxiliaries were allowed to elect delegates to future conventions and local metal trades councils. In addition, blacks henceforth would receive equal union insurance benefits. Auxiliaries nevertheless remained something less than full union locals and blacks something less than full union members. As far as Boilermaker president Charles MacGowan was concerned, the auxiliary problem was "not within the membership but with professional agitation attempting to make a cause where none exists."[34]

This was not the view of Judge Butler of the Marin Superior Court.

On February 17, 1944, Butler announced his decision in what was now known as the case of *James v. Marinship*. Butler ruled that the Boilermakers' policy of "discriminating against and segregating Negroes into auxiliaries is contrary to public policy of the state of California." He therefore prohibited the union from requiring blacks to join auxiliaries as a condition of employment and barred Marinship management from laying off workers who refused to pay auxiliary dues.[35]

Both union and management appealed the decision to the California Supreme Court, and it took nearly a year for the state's highest court to decide the case. In the meantime, the Boilermakers did not accept blacks as full members, but the union could not require auxiliary membership as a condition of employment at Marinship. Thus black employees continued working at the yard without paying union dues. Judge Butler's February 1944 decision did not apply to other yards, but cases similar to the Marinship suit were brought in various Bay Area courts throughout 1944. FEPC chairman Ross continued to seek a voluntary settlement, but the matter was not resolved until the supreme court announced its final decision on January 2, 1945.

The court's unanimous opinion, written by Chief Justice Phil Gibson, was a decisive defeat for the Boilermakers. The justices found that it was "readily apparent that the membership offered to Negroes is discriminatory and unequal." The supreme court agreed with Judge Butler that the auxiliary practice violated a California statute that held racial discrimination to be "contrary to public policy." The court explained that it was not outlawing the concept of closed shop *per se*, but that "an arbitrarily closed union is incompatible with a closed shop."[36]

The court also refused to let management off the hook. Justice Gibson swept aside Marinship's assertion that it was simply enforcing the terms of a federally approved labor contract and could not be held responsible for union discrimination. Gibson pointed out that the company had "full knowledge of the dispute and at least indirectly assisted the union in carrying out discrimination." By the same token, Local 6 could not argue that it only enforced national union policies over which it had no control. "The true rule is, of course, that the agent is liable for his acts." [37]

The *San Francisco Chronicle* hailed the decision as confirmation of the principle of "no representation, no dues." The Marin City *Marin Citizen* said the ruling "should be welcomed by every believer in genuine trade unionism," while the Communist Party's *People's World* emphasized that the court had outlawed discrimination, not the closed shop. Joseph James made the same point, contending that he and his supporters had waged the battle "strictly on a pro-union basis." By this time, James had been elected president of the San Francisco NAACP branch and proclaimed that the organization was "in the forefront of every fight against open shop proposals."[38]

At Moore shipyard in Oakland, Katherine Archibald reported that the union's initial 1943 victory in federal court had "aroused the rejoicing of several of my [white] colleagues." But the final state supreme court decision in 1945 gave blacks "status as a people in the eyes of their white companions." There might be mutterings of discontent, "but the decision was respected and the conviction grew that the law at least . . . was on the side of the black man." One white worker conceded, "I guess we can't keep hold of all the jobs."[39]

The union announced it would obey the decision and abolish its California auxiliaries. But in their place, the Boilermakers intended to form "separate but equal" local lodges. Blacks would be given full membership rights but would be required to join all-black locals. Whether this would have passed the judicial test will never be known, since the union made serious efforts to establish "separate but equal" locals for only a short time. A 1948 study found that all Boilermaker lodges in the Bay Area were racially integrated.[40]

James v. Marinship therefore produced important changes in Boilermaker membership practices. Ironically, however, very few blacks were able to take advantage of these changes. As Marinship worker Moses Beard put it, by the time of the court decision, "we were on the way out."[41]

In 1944, Local 6 had 36,000 members, including about 3,000 blacks theoretically in segregated auxiliaries. By 1948, the union was racially integrated but had only 1,800 members, of whom just 150 were black. Even by the time of the supreme court decision, work was declining at Marinship and other Bay Area yards. The allies were clearly winning the war, and the government began cutting back contracts. Between January 1944 and January 1945, total Bay Area shipyard employment fell from about 240,000 to 200,000. Black employment in the yards continued to increase during that year (from 24,000 to 26,000), but after January 1945, the black work force also rapidly declined. There were 20,000 black shipyard workers in July, 12,000 in September and an "insignificant number" by the time Marinship formally closed in May 1946.[42]

Talented Marinship workers often performed at yard shows and launching ceremonies.

It was a classic case of "last hired, first fired." During the war, about 75 percent of San Francisco black heads of households were classified as skilled industrial workers, the great majority of them in the shipyards. By 1948, only about 25 percent of black workers were still in industrial jobs, while over half were employed as unskilled laborers or service workers. More than 15 percent of Bay Area black men were unemployed in 1948, nearly three times the state-wide rate for all persons. The United States Department of Employment noted that "as long as Negroes are commonly regarded as marginal labor, they will suffer very heavy unemployment when sufficient white labor is available."[43]

Given this situation, it was hardly surprising that some blacks left the Bay Area after the war, including Joseph James who returned to New York to pursue his singing career. Yet an estimated 85 percent of the wartime migrants stayed, their numbers increased by their newborn children and by new, postwar migration from the South. By 1950, San Francisco's black population had grown to over 40,000. By 1960, it was nearly 75,000. As Lester Granger of the Urban League had warned, much of the Fillmore became a black "ghetto." And so did Marin City, surrounded by some of the most prosperous white suburbs in American.[44]

The postwar problems of black poverty, unemployment and lack of economic opportunity have become chronic for a large portion of the region's non-white population. Of course, this situation is by no means unique to the Bay Area. But the area's experience is unusual in that the beginnings of its large black population were so directly tied to a short-term boom in a single industry. As long as the wartime shipyards operated at or near capacity, blacks had access to well-paying jobs. In the midst of the national emergency and regional labor shortage, Marinship blacks even won the legal principle of equal membership in exclusive craft unions. But the precipitous decline of the shipyards after the war was an economic disaster from which the region's African American population has never fully recovered. Even the protests, civil rights legislation and anti-poverty measures of the 1960s did not produce economic opportunity comparable to World War II.

In 1945 Joseph James believed he had identified a pattern in California's treatment of minority migrants: "We need them, we use them, when we are through with them, we banish them."[45] Wartime blacks were needed and used, but not banished. Thousands still live in the Bay Area, including some former Marinship workers still residing in Marin City. During the 1940s these men and women won battles that established important legal principles, but blacks have yet to win an equitable share of the region's wealth and power.

CHAPTER EIGHT

Marin City

IN 1942, ALICE PHILLIPS ROSE, A social worker for the USO-Travelers Aid Service (which provided assistance to newly arrived war workers), argued that small West Coast towns were "in no position to assimilate" a vast influx of new residents. "In the small town, the newcomer stands out in base relief against the background of established customs in the community. . . . He is received not as a proud war worker, but as a competitor for rationed supplies." Rose noted that townspeople often referred to the new arrivals as "Okies" and "Arkies" and considered them "a group of labor profiteers."[1]

Sausalito was one of the small communities most dramatically affected by the wartime influx. By January 1943, less than nine months after Marinship began operations, the Sausalito area population already had grown to nearly 7,000, almost double the prewar total. For most residents, the change seemed "to happen overnight."[2] The town certainly became livelier. One former Marinship worker recalled that Sausalito had 13 bars, and "they were a lot of fun, too." Another former worker remembered Sausalito as a town "that never slept." but with increased night life came increased disorder. In the month of March 1942, before the yard began operations, the Sausalito jail booked just three prisoners. By September, the figure had risen to 27; by March 1943, it was 81. Guy MacVicar of the yard's recruiting office was happy to see the streets "filled with cars bearing license plates from the Middle West and the South," but for many Sausalitans, the changes experienced by their small town were a "dark portent of things to come."[3]

Of all the problems caused by the great migration, the most immediate and obvious was a housing shortage. In response to the emergency,
the National Housing Authority coordinated a vast regional construction
effort on the West Coast. In cooperation with the Maritime Commission,
the federal Public Housing Authority, another former New Deal agency,
allocated funds to employers and local communities for specific
projects. Marinship executives learned in early June 1942 that approval
was possible for such a project in or around Sausalito. Working with
local officials of the Housing Authority of Marin County, which had
been established a few months earlier in hopes of attracting federal
funds, the company took just three days to come up with a general plan
for a new community called Marin City on a site just north of the yard
and the Sausalito city limits.[4]

Marin City was to include 1,500 family units: 700 apartments and
800 detached or semi-detached homes. Nearby were dormitories for
more than 1,000 single workers. Although the company would assist in
the construction of facilities, the Marin Housing Authority was to own
and operate the project. On June 8, 1942 federal officials formally
approved the proposal, and from then on, according to Marinship's
housing supervisor, "it was a race between construction of the shipyard
and the housing."[5] Initial housing applications were accepted at the
beginning of August, and the first family moved into a completed
apartment on the 18th. By the time Marin City was officially dedicated
in September, nearly all the apartments were ready for occupancy and
duplexes were being completed at the rate of 30 per day. In January
1943, 2,600 people lived in the family units with another 1,000 in dormitories. By the end of the year, Marin City's population was nearly 6,000,
making it Marin County's second-largest community, with almost twice
as many people as prewar Sausalito.[6]

Monthly rents varied from $29 for a one-room apartment to $43.50
for a detached six-room house. The weekly dormitory rate was $5.50.
Rents included utilities and medical care provided by the California
Physicians Service. Although the dormitories were initially filled,
vacancies occurred as worker's families arrived in the Bay Area. On the
other hand, demand for family housing grew steadily, and waiting lists
continued to exist until the summer of 1945.[7]

The family units were built on a hill overlooking the Bay, with
project streets designed to follow the site's contours. Local architect Carl
Grommé and his staff adapted standard federal housing designs to

MARIN CITY ... HOMES FOR MARINSHIP WORKERS

Layout for a company brochure, touting partially completed Marin City.

conform to the hillside location, taking advantage of views and support-
ing some of the structures with long, exposed struts so that they became
popularly known as "pole houses." Although it was planned as a
temporary wartime project, the *San Francisco Chronicle* noted the
buildings were constructed "of redwood, to last."

The architects also designed community and commercial buildings
on the flatlands in front of the hillside housing units. Eventually, Marin
City had its own post office, library, community hall and elementary and
nursery schools, as well as barber and beauty shops, shoe repair, laundry
and dry cleaning establishments, and stores selling groceries, drugs,
beverages and general merchandise. The dormitory complex included a
cafeteria and gymnasium. Perhaps the most notable building was the
elementary school, a low structure with classrooms opening onto
outdoor walkways and courtyards. It became a prototype for much of the
California public school architecture of the postwar era.

Author and planner Mel Scott probably spoke for many Bay Area
residents when he regretted that Marin City's development had come at
the expense of some of the area's "most beautiful meadows and
surrounding hills." Nevertheless, he noted that the project had been
"outstanding among war born developments, both in planning and in
community facilities."[8]

Most Marinship workers were unable to take advantage of these
amenities. At its height, Marin City only accommodated 12 to 15
percent of the yard's work force. Other workers had to compete for the
limited supply of available private housing. Even in the best of circumstances, the great migration would have strained the region's housing
market, but with wartime controls on private construction, the shortage
of dwellings became especially acute. Federal authorities allowed Marin
contractors to build more than 800 FHA-supported small private homes,
but this did not begin to meet the demand. Some Marinship workers
were forced to live for a time in trailers, garages and even chicken
coops. During the rapid buildup of the labor force in the summer of
1944, the company erected tents for temporary housing. Marinship also
appealed to local families to rent space to the newcomers. Some
weekend cabins in the county's rural west side were made available, and
residents often rented out spare rooms. The results were not always
satisfactory. One Sausalito woman rented a room to what she thought
were a husband and wife. But the couple moved in with three children,
several relatives and *their* children. By the time the renters were

evicted, 18 people were living in the three-bedroom house.[9]

By early 1943, about 5,000 Marinship workers lived in Marin County or the adjoining portions of southern Sonoma County. About 2,000 additional employees found housing in other Bay Area suburban communities, but the majority of the yard's work force, over 10,000 individuals, lived in San Francisco. During the war, the city's population grew by about 25 percent as it became, in Mel Scott's words, "a dormitory metropolis." From the yard's earliest days, Marinship planners had expected San Francisco's large stock of residential hotels, boarding houses and apartments to accommodate the bulk of the yard's workers.[10] But workers living in San Francisco and elsewhere had to get to Sausalito efficiently and in a manner that would not strain the nation's heavily rationed supplies of gas and rubber.

Until the mid-1930s, Sausalito had been effectively served by regular ferry service to San Francisco and an electric rail system that covered much of southern Marin County. Completion of the Golden Gate Bridge in 1937 encouraged the use of private autos, and by 1942 both the rail and ferry systems had ceased operations. Pacific Greyhound provided bus service to San Francisco and parts of Marin, so Marinship management asked the company to expand service to and from the yard. Marinship offered a per rider subsidy, but the bus company held out for a guaranteed monthly payment. When the yard began negotiations with another firm, however, Greyhound came to terms and provided substantial service from San Francisco and various points in Marin and southern Sonoma County. Greyhound particularly had large numbers of pick-up points throughout San Francisco. One former worker who lived in the Sunset district remembered taking a trolley to 19th Avenue, where he caught the bus to the yard via the Golden Gate Bridge, a commute of about 40 minutes.[11]

The Maritime Commission also provided funds to restore ferry service from San Francisco to Sausalito. The ferryboat *Sierra Nevada* began operations in mid-1942 and carried more than one million individual passengers before its last voyage in 1945. The craft had only one serious mishap: during a heavy fog it became entangled in the net that protected San Francisco Bay from submarine attack.[12]

By the fall of 1943, the special buses were carrying about 3,300 workers per day and the ferry was serving an additional 1,800. In addition, many employees walked to the yard from Marin City and Sausalito. Nevertheless, more than 10,000 people were still commuting

Marin City fully occupied. Multi-unit apartments and public buildings are on the lower elevations. Smaller living units and "pole houses" are on the higher hillsides.

by private automobile. To reduce traffic and conserve gas and rubber, Marinship encouraged carpooling. The Golden Gate Bridge District offered special reduced-rate tolls for carpoolers and sold commute tickets right at the yard. These efforts to encourage carpooling were so successful that Marinship auto commuters averaged 4.2 persons per car.[13]

The majority of Marinship workers may have lived in San Francisco, but Marin City still attracted national attention as a highly successful model project. In 1943, for example, Massachusetts Congressman George Bates proclaimed Marin City "the best administered and best organized war housing project that I have seen." Bates had visited "hundreds of war housing projects" as a member of the House Naval Affairs Subcommittee and said he had seen "none that so ideally meets the requirements of a community of war workers" as Marin City.[14]

Most of the credit for Marin City's well-publicized accomplishments went to the Housing Authority of Marin County. The authority was chaired by Ernest White, president of the Marin Central Labor Council, but the agency's moving spirit was executive director Guy Ciocca. A Marin County lawyer and police judge, Ciocca was well-connected politically and determined to run a successful project. He was ably assisted by his chief of project services, Milen Dempster, an experienced community organizer and project manager who had been a Socialist Party candidate for California governor and manager of a federal migrant labor camp. Applying his reformist principles to Marin City, he worked to assure that a full range of social services would be available to residents. For example, Dempster cooperated with Alice Phillips Rose to establish a USO-Travelers Aid Service office at Marin City. The office provided a variety of services to new arrivals, including short-term loans to tide families over until the first paycheck. (Rose persuaded Marinship management to subsidize the loan program.)[15]

Dempster was largely responsible for the project's famous non-discrimination policy. While blacks were accepted into wartime housing projects throughout the Bay Area, they were generally segregated into all-black apartment and dormitory units. At Marin City, however, Dempster rented on a first-come, first-served basis without regard to race. The result was probably the most thoroughly integrated project in the nation. Marin City also had an active Double V Club, a predominately black organization committed to a "double victory" over racism at home and fascism overseas.[16]

Dempster admitted that Marin City's biracial environment sometimes led to conflict and to complaints by "prejudiced whites." He responded to the complaints by pointing out that "these black men are Americans. They are needed just as you are—to build ships." Dempster believed that "gradually the color prejudices lost ground." The *San Francisco Chronicle* agreed and hoped "that the lessons we have all learned at Marin City will be carried to other parts of the nation." The *Christian Science Monitor* reported that Marin City's experience proved that "white people and Negroes can live side by side—and get along." But a former Housing Authority official admitted that if the white majority at Marin City were given the power to eject blacks from the project, "they probably would do so."[17]

Marin City was unincorporated territory under direct Housing Authority control, but in the spring of 1943 the authority encouraged the establishment of an elected "city council" with advisory powers. A community meeting of about 150 residents approved a constitution calling for a 13-member council elected from four voting districts. All residents 18 years or older could vote in council elections. The council would also include non-voting representatives of the Housing Authority and various community groups. Twenty-nine candidates filed for the April 22 elections, and voters chose a council that included black and female representation. On July 16, the council published the first issue of the *Marin Citizen*, a weekly newspaper that was both a source of general community information and a house organ for the council majority.[18]

Probably the most influential member of the council was Michael Smith, a Marinship worker from Washington state, where he had been a leader of the Democratic Party and served in the legislature. During Smith's term as council president, the body generally supported the Housing Authority's reformist policies, including its strong non-discrimination stand. The council, for example, refused to seat a non-voting representative of the Marin City Women's Club until that organization allowed black members. The *Citizen* editorially supported the black workers' cause against the Boilermakers union, arguing that "equal treatment for all" was the "best guarantee against racial trouble."[19]

Neither the council nor the newspaper, however, hesitated to point out community shortcomings and criticize the Housing Authority. The *Citizen* echoed the common complaints about the poor drainage system that turned Marin City's flatlands into a veritable swamp during the winter rainy season. "Hog Hollow," some called it. The paper reported the story of Herman Campbell, "the swimming councilman," who fell into a ditch after a council meeting. "I heard a splash," one witness said, "and looked down to see Campbell swimming down the sidewalk."[20]

On a more serious note, the *Citizen* also criticized improper conduct by the "Marin City Police Department," four county deputy sheriffs paid by the Housing Authority. In August 1943 the *Citizen* argued for changes in police "attitudes and actions," towards blacks and teenagers, who, the paper claimed, were treated like "they were some sort of second-class citizens." In October the *Citizen* again lashed out at the police in a front-page editorial entitled "NO GESTAPO WANTED HERE!" After the paper criticized the county sheriff and Housing Authority director Ciocca for refusing to take action, both men attended a community meeting and apparently promised some improvements. But the problems persisted and in January 1945, the *Citizen* was still reporting charges of police brutality, this time in the case of a mental patient being transported from Marin City to the county jail in San Rafael. The deputies claimed they injured the man inadvertently while defending themselves. Michael Smith pointed out, however, that they "defended themselves all over the face, head and hands of the patient—and emerged unscathed." [21]

Despite these problems, Marin City residents needed and wanted police protection. Like many Bay Area communities, the project had a growing crime rate and a particularly distressing problem of juvenile delinquency. The war effort had disrupted normal family life, and young people from all over the country were thrown together in places such as Marin City. Able to earn good wages, teenagers often left school and sometimes formed troublesome gangs. The USO-Travelers Aid Service urged Marinship not to hire young teens, noting that students were dropping out of nearby Tamalpais High School to work in the yard. The service also charged that "older men" were "exploiting young boys in gambling and drinking" in the Marin City dormitories. In late 1943, the Housing Authority promoted the establishment of an elected youth council "to counter teen destructiveness." But in the summer of 1945, the *Citizen* was still reporting problems caused by teenaged gangs. [22]

The *Citizen* also criticized some of the merchants in the Marin City commercial complex for violating federal price standards. Such violations, as well as other forms of profiteering and black market activity, were common in the tightly regulated wartime economy. In January 1944, Michael Smith and five other project residents sued Waldo's Marin City Market, alleging price control violations. Market owner Waldo Giacomini denied the charges and claimed he was the victim of a conspiracy by the city council and the *Citizen*. In court he argued that he had always treated his customers and employees "like white men," a phrase that hardly endeared him to the black residents attending the hearing. The judge ruled in favor of the plaintiffs, and in February the Housing Authority evicted Giacomini from the project after federal authorities found him guilty of more than 20 additional price violations. Apparently the situation did not substantially improve, however. In November, federal officials announced that the new operators of the market were also guilty of "numerous price violations." [23]

The city council suffered its greatest defeat by involving itself in Sausalito politics. Although Marin City was located outside of the Sausalito city limits, the project was within the boundaries of the town's

elementary school district. By October 1942 more than 50 new Marin
City students had already forced Sausalito's Central School into double
sessions. The crowding continued until the project's own school opened
in the spring of 1943. By autumn, the Marin City Elementary School
was the largest in the county, enrolling 800 of the Sausalito district's
1,300 students. The project was also home for about two-thirds of the
district's residents, yet all members of the elected school board were
old-time Sausalito citizens.[24]

In August 1943, a board member resigned, and the *Citizen* urged
appointment of a Marin City resident to fill the vacant seat until the next
election. The county school superintendent, however, chose a Sausalitan
who was supported by existing board members. The superintendent
added insult to injury by observing that he doubted "whether there was
anyone in Marin City who could even qualify" for the job. For the
Citizen, this comment displayed an all-too-familiar attitude. The paper
charged that old-time residents "didn't want shipyard workers here in
the first place and now . . . are doing their best to make our stay here
uncomfortable." Sausalito was treating Marin city "as if it were some
kind of a government concentration camp."

The *Citizen* admitted that some "far seeing" Marin County
residents welcomed the new arrivals but argued that, in general, Marin
City was badly treated. The paper advised project residents to use their
votes to change the situation. While the *Citizen* claimed to be
non-partisan on most political matters, "as far as the welfare of our town
and our people are concerned . . . we are as partisan as can be."[25]

In March 1944 the newspaper announced the candidacy of Dan Allen, a Marin City Council member, for a seat on the Sausalito school
board in the upcoming spring election. A yard shipfitter and two-year
Marin City resident, Allen was a former teacher who had attended Yale
and Stanford. He was opposed by incumbent Robert Anderson in a race
that generally divided the school district along Sausalito-Marin City
lines. In April, the *Sausalito News*, which had previously criticized
old-time residents for calling Marin City "Okieville," began a special
Marin City edition. The stated purpose of the new publication was to
"present ALL the news without favor." The *Citizen* argued, however,
that the new edition of the *News* represented "an attack by outside
interests." Michael Smith wrote that "the Sausalito Chamber of
Commerce is behind this outside paper" and warned local businessmen
that "anyone who seeks to undermine the *Marin Citizen* and our Marin

City Council will face the wrath of our community."[26]

Anderson, nevertheless, had some support in Marin City. At a candidates meeting in the project community hall, one member of the audience accused Smith and his associates of being "the political bosses of Marin City." Smith denied the charge and continued his strong support of Allen. He argued that prominent Sausalitans attacked the candidate because "he lives on the wrong side of the tracks. . . . Just the thought of anyone from Marin City being elected is too painful for them to contemplate." On election day, May 19, 1944, the *Citizen* ran a banner headline: "ELECT DAN ALLEN!"[27]

Allen was easily defeated, 676 votes to 307, however. Anderson won Sausalito by a huge margin, 583 to 110, but Allen's victory in Marin City was far closer, 197 to 93. Significantly, more than 800 Marin City residents did not bother to vote at all. (Six months later, in the national presidential election, over 1,200 Marin Cityites cast ballots, favoring Roosevelt over Dewey by a 3-to-1 margin.)[28] In spite of tremendous efforts by the *Citizen* and the city council, most project residents apparently felt little stake in the outcome of the local school board election.

Similarly, most residents seemed to ignore the council's other activities. The *Citizen* routinely reported poor turnouts in council elections, and council seats were often uncontested.[29] Of course, the body's power was limited, and residents may have reasonably concluded that Marin City elections did not count for much. In addition, the population of the community was constantly changing as families moved in and out. For most residents, "home" was somewhere else. Despite Milen Dempster's efforts at fostering community feeling and participation, few were willing to invest their time or interest in local affairs.

In April 1945, the *Citizen* reported that Michael Smith had left for military service; apparently his deferment had run out. In May, the paper also announced that Milen Dempster, "the moving force behind many of the accomplishments in Marin City," had resigned to accept a United Nations post in Germany.[30] In the war's last months, then, Marin City lost the two men who tried hardest to bring civic involvement and self-government to the project.

Wartime production and employment began to wind down in early 1945. In the fall of 1944, demand for housing had been so great that the Housing Authority had limited Marin City residency to families with at least one member employed at Marinship or six smaller local defense contractors. By May 1945, however, the project was open to everyone working in "essential industries" in Marin or San Francisco counties. In effect, explained one Housing Authority official, "practically anyone working is eligible to live here." In addition, terminated Marinship workers could stay in the project "for a reasonable time." Marin City was still full, but for the first time since 1942, there was no waiting list. After the Japanese surrender in August, the *Citizen* reported that the community's future was "undecided."[31]

Marin City did, in fact, survive as Marin County's major public housing project. As white residents gradually moved out, finding new homes and jobs throughout the area, the bulk of the project's population became black. After Marinship closed, many residents were unemployed or forced to take low-paying jobs. Leon Samuels, for example, worked for more than 30 years as a janitor and gardener after the yard shut down. In 1986, he and his family had lived in Marin City for more than four decades.[32] Those residents who could afford to move out were often unable to do so because of endemic housing discrimination.

In the early 1960s, the temporary wooden apartments were torn down and partially replaced by large concrete buildings. Some residents were also allowed to buy the single-family pole houses, but redevelopment caused an overall decline in the project's population. Later in the decade, racial conflicts over integration and "community control" raged in the Sausalito school district. Construction of expensive condominiums in the hills above the project during the 1970s and 1980s seemed to reinforce the sense of racial division between Marin City and the rest of the largely white, suburban county. In 1986, Thelma McKinney, another former Marinship worker and long-time Marin City resident, believed that while overt racial discrimination had declined, economic hardship had not. "Now we can move out," she exclaimed, "but we can't afford to." McKinney said she didn't "see any improvement. . . . I see only regression."[33]

Not all Marin City residents were as pessimistic as Thelma McKinney, and the 1980s did see ambitious plans to rebuild the project's long-abandoned commercial complex. But of all the legacies of Marinship, Marin City is the saddest.

To the extent that the project ever lived up to its image as a model community, it was due to the special economic and social circumstances of World War II. Once the wartime economic boom and housing shortage ended, traditional American racial and class divisions reasserted themselves. Far from being a model, Marin City became an all-too-typical low-income housing project suffering from the long-term effects of racism and poverty. Like the newly arrived war workers before them, Marin City's postwar residents were never fully accepted into the mainstream of Marin County society. As Alice Phillips Rose put it in 1942, they continued "to stand out in base relief against the established customs" of the surrounding community.[34]

CHAPTER NINE

Shutdown

"ONE DAY THE SHIFT DIDN'T change." That was the way former general manager Bill Waste remembered Marinship's end of operations on May 16, 1946. "The job was done," said Waste. "Just like any other construction job that starts as a project and ends that way—like Boulder Dam, the Bay Bridge, a big pipeline, or any oil refinery." Kenneth Bechtel agreed: "The shipyard was originally expected to be 'expendable,' and its cost charged off to the war like a decommissioned battleship or airport which has outlived its usefulness."[1]

Members of the Bechtel Corporation, with its long heritage of construction work, naturally viewed Marinship in that light. Company executives were used to thinking of their careers as a series of discreet projects. When one job was finished, you went on to the next. But Marinship was different. It was a vast industrial enterprise producing finished goods rather than a construction project building physical facilities. Marinship employees comprised an industrial work force, and many of them hoped to keep their jobs after the war. For that reason, management never referred to the yard as "expendable" during the war years. Instead, company executives continually discussed the possibility of postwar operations and tried to use this possibility to promote worker loyalty and efficiency.

One of the first press discussions of the shipbuilding industry's postwar future appeared in the April 30, 1943 edition of the *San Francisco Chronicle*. Reporter Milton Silverman predicted that only two West Coast Maritime Commission yards would survive: Henry Kaiser's Richmond #3 and his Swan Island facility in Portland. Marinship officials disagreed. "Don't count us out," they told Silverman. "We'll be in there as one of the top two or three."[2] In June, Kenneth Bechtel made much the same point to a congressional committee, testifying that Marinship and Kaiser #3 had "great prospects of continuation."[3]

The Maritime Commission apparently also believed that the yard had a postwar future, for in May 1943, commission chairman Emory Land told Marinship workers that they had "a better chance to endure permanently than most of the rest of the yards. . . . You've got the best yard in the world. You have the best climate, the best environment. . . . This is a shipyard that ought to endure. These are homes that you have, an environment that you have that ought to endure." A year later, Land's chief assistant, Admiral Howard Vickery, called Marinship "a high efficiency yard." It might be impossible to keep the largest commission facilities operating after the war, but Vickery described Marinship as "what we consider a small yard, ideally situated."[4]

Marinship managers consistently tried to convince workers that greater production and efficiency would help secure the yard's postwar existence. In the August 20, 1943 *Marin-er*, Bill Waste wrote that costs had to be reduced because "no company can give continuity of employment unless the product is sold." On March 18, 1944, Waste claimed that "in the future, shipyards that get the business will be those that produce at the lowest cost." One year later, Kenneth Bechtel told employees that Marinship was now "in the major shipbuilding league." "Our future," he argued, "like any other major leaguer, depends on how efficiently we play the game."[5]

That future became a matter of particular concern in 1945, as wartime production began winding down. In February, Marinship announced a gradual phase-out of the swing and graveyard shifts, concentrating work during the daylight hours. Management emphasized that the resulting decline in workers would occur by attrition rather than layoff, but the *Marin Citizen* noted that the change would deprive many employees of their late-shift bonuses. By March 1945, the yard work force had shrunk to 11,500, only about half the peak employment figure of 1943–44. The War Manpower Commission predicted (accurately as it turned out) that only 600 people would be working at the yard by the end of the year.[6]

Crane lowers one of the army barges built for the planned invasion of Japan.

Marinship was by no means the only Bay Area plant reducing its labor force in the spring of 1945. In April, the *Chronicle* announced that "the shipyard gold rush is over. . . . Like the gold rush of '49 the golden era of shipbuilding on San Francisco Bay has slipped into history." The article concluded that the most secure jobs were not in yards such as Marinship, which specialized in new construction, but in Navy facilities like Mare Island and Hunters Point, which also emphasized ship repair.[7] Apparently, many Marinship workers agreed, and in May, Bill Waste had to use the yard's public address system to plead with experienced specialists not to leave Marinship for jobs in the Navy yards. In the pages of *The Marin-er*, Waste continued to hold out hope for a postwar future: "Surely, nothing could be more desirable . . . than a transition from a wartime activity to some peacetime function for Marinship." But in May, President Truman ordered cancellation of $7 billion in shipyard contracts, including orders for five of nine outstanding Marinship tankers.[8]

Then in June and July, the yard's prospects seemed miraculously to revive. The Maritime Commission announced that Marinship would start ship repair work and the Army and Navy awarded the company lucrative contracts to build barges for the projected invasion of Japan. Marinship was suddenly hiring again. "Workers in all shipyard crafts are urgently needed," Bill Waste announced. The Kaiser yards received similar contracts, and the *Chronicle* speculated that barge construction might have the effect of stopping "possibly until 1946—the declining rate of employment in Bay Area shipyards." A Marinship executive noted that "recent pessimistic rumors were like the reports of Mark Twain's death. . . . To say the least, they were exaggerated."[9]

The bubble burst, however, when Japan surrendered in August. The Army and Navy halted further barge construction, and the Maritime Commission canceled another half-billion dollars in contracts, including orders for two of the remaining four Marinship tankers. In *The Mariner*, Bill Waste tried to keep up an optimistic front, but when the yard delivered its last ship on October 28, the *Chronicle* accurately reported that "Marinship's work is done." By November the labor force had indeed declined to 600, and even yard executives were openly pessimistic about the future. Kenneth Bechtel pointed out that "the nation's shipbuilding and repair capacity far exceeds peacetime needs."[10]

The Maritime Commission was in fact willing to allow Marinship to continue postwar operations under Bechtel management, but Kenneth Bechtel explained that "we did not want to operate a government-owned facility in competition with privately-owned plants after the war." The commission also offered to sell the yard to the company, but Bechtel said that "it had become clear to us that this would serve neither public nor private interests." The Sausalito site was thus turned over to the Army Corps of Engineers as an operating center for its Pacific Island Reconstruction Program.[11] Eventually, the Corps needed only a small portion of the plant (including the warehouse building that now houses the Bay Model and the Marinship Museum).

The rest of the property was sold to private parties and has evolved into a wildly diverse waterfront, including small manufacturing and water-related businesses, sleek office complexes, recreational marinas, commercial fishing terminals and a variety of houseboats, ranging in character from luxury to handmade-funky. Calship in Southern California was also closed, and so, by mid-1946, The Bechtel Corporation had withdrawn from its manufacturing enterprises and was once again a pure construction and engineering firm. For company managers "it was on to the next job."

Frederic Lane, the major historian of the Maritime Commission's wartime construction effort, has concluded that the program was a success because it produced ships "with unparalleled speed."[12] By that standard, Marinship was one of the commission's star performers. Given the yard's late start and difficult transition to tanker production, 93 ships in three-and-one-half years was a remarkable record. One Marinship tanker was sunk by enemy action and eight of the yard's Navy oilers were part of the fleet that accepted the Japanese surrender in Tokyo Bay. The yard's first ship, the Liberty *William Richardson*, made nine separate voyages during the war, covering 102,000 miles. Its maiden trip began in San Francisco in November 1942 and covered 13,000 miles, to New York via Wellington, New Zealand and Melbourne, Australia. After the war, the *Richardson* was fitted as a transport to carry soldiers home, and one of those soldiers was amazed to find a picture of his cousin in the ship's wardroom. It turned out that the cousin had been the sponsor at the *Richardson*'s Sausalito launching.[13]

Marinship's success, however, cannot be measured only by the ships it produced and the voyages they completed. As a profitable and well-publicized venture, the yard also contributed to the development of the Bechtel Company and strengthened the corporation's reputation as a "can-do" organization. Marinship, along with Calship and the other wartime projects, greatly enhanced Bechtel's Washington ties, and, in one writer's words, won the company "friends in high places." After the war, John McCone, former Bechtel executive, Calship president and Marinship board member, occupied a number of powerful public posts, including Atomic Energy Commission chairman and director of the CIA. In the 1980s, two other former company men, George Shultz and Caspar Weinberger, served in the Reagan cabinet, as Secretary of State and Secretary of Defense respectively.[14]

As American political and military influence grew in the war and postwar eras, so did the scope of Bechtel operations. The wartime visits of Saudi princes to the Marinship yard, for example, heralded the company's substantial new role in the Middle East. Bechtel's dramatic rise in economic and political influence was part of a larger process through which California firms became major players in worldwide business and finance. The war certainly did not begin the industrialization of California: that had occurred decades before. But World War II greatly expanded the size and scope of the state's enterprises. And like many of California's largest businesses, Bechtel was a charter member of what Dwight Eisenhower called the "military-industrial complex" that had been spawned by World War II.

Several former Marinship executives went on to play important roles in the corporation's expanding operations. Engineer Russ Quick later described how he "built pipelines all over the world." Ray Hamilton, Robert Digges, and Jack Chambers were among the other Marinship

A visit by members of the Saudi royal family presages the Bechtel Company's postwar international importance. William Waste and Kenneth Bechtel are on the right.

managers who stayed with Bechtel. Robert Bridges went into private law practice and in that capacity served as Bechtel's powerful chief attorney. Kenneth Bechtel continued as a member of the corporation's board of directors and remained active in the company's insurance subsidiary. But in corporate affairs, he continued to be overshadowed by his dynamic brother Steve. Bill Waste also remained a part of the Bechtel hierarchy, reaching the post of executive vice president before retiring in the 1960s.

The most remarkable case of corporate mobility involved John O'Connell, the former Marinship labor coordinator. The one-time high school industrial arts teacher and counselor from Richmond eventually became the company's chief labor negotiator and corporate vice chairman. O'Connell cultivated close ties with important political and labor leaders, including AFL-CIO president George Meany. He also played a significant role in maintaining Bechtel's Saudi connection. O'Connell became known within the company as "Mr. Full Charge."[15]

Unlike the executives, the great majority of regular Marinship workers had no chance of continued employment with Bechtel. After the war, Bill Waste said that he had so much confidence in the abilities of the wartime work force that "I don't think we have to worry about the men and women who checked in and out of the yard."[16] But the prospects for laid-off workers seemed problematical at best in immediate postwar America. Defense plants were closing and millions of service men and women were returning to the civilian labor market. National unemployment doubled in 1946, and prices increased by 30 percent as wartime controls were removed. The Japanese surrender had been so sudden and the demobilization so rapid that plans for peacetime economic conversion were overwhelmed by events.[17]

Fortunately, wartime high wages and full employment had produced a great deal of pent-up consumer demand that was released at the end of the conflict. While the war brought widespread destruction to the economies of many industrial countries, it strengthened and consolidated America's manufacturing system, thus enhancing the nation's competitive position. California's economy, in particular, continued its rapid expansion after only a brief pause.

In this environment, most former Marinship employees soon found new jobs, and some even took advantage of new economic opportunities. Sam Knoles had hoped to stay on with Bechtel, but when he received his pink slip, he restarted his former sheet metal business and built it into a prosperous enterprise. Dick Miller had been a musician before the war. After leaving Marinship, he used his knowledge of the entertainment industry to open a San Francisco night club. Some former women employees like Josephine Doyle returned to their prewar roles as homemakers, while others stayed in the labor force, only now in typical "women's jobs." Mary Poole had loved working as a welder: "It was a wonderful job. . . . I didn't know anything until I went to work at Marinship." But after the yard closed, she went back to her more "traditional" career as a teacher.

As we have seen, blacks had by far the most difficult time finding new employment, and when they did, it was often at rock-bottom wages. Cy Record told the story of one former black shipyard worker who had been making $10 a day during the war. By 1946 he considered himself lucky to be earning $6.40 as a laborer. Given postwar inflation, his real income was less than half what it had been in the war years.[18]

Some Marinship employees managed to stay on until the very end. Carpenter Edward Winkler was among the first to be hired to build the yard in 1942. In 1946, he was still at Marinship, crating up invasion barges that had never been launched. Cafeteria supervisor Grace Pastori locked the dining room door for the last time at midnight on May 16, 1946, when the Corps of Engineers formally took possession of the yard. "It was a sad time," she recalled. "It was eerie seeing so much stillness where there had been so much action." Kenneth Bechtel was also on hand for the transfer of property. He remembered that "when the time came for passing over to the Army, nothing outwardly changed, but I realized that Marinship as we knew it had become history . . . ."[19]

Marinship now lives on most vividly in the memories of the men and women who worked there. Most ex-workers remember sharing a strong sense of common purpose and accomplishment. It existed in spite of much "goofing off" and shirking. It even survived the incipient, serious conflicts between labor and management, men and women, and blacks and whites. Camille Almada recalls "everybody working together." Harold Elberg says "it was a good time . . . America at its best." Leon Samuels mentions "good relations between people," while Gerald Carlton claims "It was fun . . . it was a *good* job." Walter Brown remembers "a lot of laughing." Camille Almada also recalls "laughing together." "It was a fun time," she says, "Of course, we were young . . . ."[20]

War was the ultimate bond that kept Marinship's diverse work force together. The war effort was the overriding purpose that explains the yard's magnificent accomplishments in construction and production and the vast resources expended to achieve these ends. Never, before or since, have the American people been so united in a common effort as they were in World War II. The irony is that so much death and destruction could motivate people to accomplish such feats of cooperation and production.

Former Marinship asbestos worker Camille Almada says, "I've changed my mind about wars. I think we should concentrate on peace."[21] All of us who share that sentiment must hope that the quest for peace can somehow become a motivating force as powerful as war, a common human purpose that will move people to produce accomplishments, which, in their own way, are as impressive as the achievements of the men and women of Marinship.

Launching of Marinship's final vessel, the tanker *Mission San Francisco*, October 1945. Signs proclaim the yard's remarkable production record.

Notes

CHAPTER 1

1. *San Francisco Chronicle*, March 23, 1942.
2. Gerald Nash, *The American West Transformed: the Impact of the Second World War* (Bloomington: U. of Indiana, 1985), viii, 19, 25.
3. Nash, 66–67; *Chronicle*, April 28, 1945.
4. For background of Bay Area maritime development, see Robert Schwendinger, *International Port of Call: an Illustrated Maritime History of the Golden Gate* (Woodland Hills, Ca: Windsor, 1984) and John H. Kemble, *San Francisco Bay: a Pictorial Maritime History* (Cambridge, Md: Cornell, 1957).
5. United States Department of Labor, Bureau of Labor Statistics, *Wartime Employment, Production, and Conditions of Work in Shipyards* (Washington: Bulletin 824, 1945), 1–6.
6. *The Kaiser Story* (Oakland: Kaiser Industries, 1968), 27–28.
7. Richard Finnie, *Marinship: the History of a Wartime Shipyard* (San Francisco: Marinship, 1947), 1–4; *Chronicle*, Nov. 1, 1942.
8. Finnie, 11–22.
9. Finnie, 7, 371.
10. Eliot Janeway, *The Struggle for Survival: a Chronicle of Economic Mobilization in World War II* (New Haven: Yale, 1951), 25.

CHAPTER 2

1. Robert Ingram, *The Bechtel Story: Seventy Years of Accomplishment in Engineering and Construction* (San Francisco: Bechtel, 1968), 1–2, and *A Builder and His Family* (San Francisco: Bechtel, 1949), 1–3.
2. Ingram, (1949), 19–27.
3. Ingram, (1949), 30–34; (1968), 6; Peter Wiley and Robert Gotlieb, *Empires in the Sun: the Rise of the New American West* (New York: Putnam, 1982), 16; *The Kaiser Story* (Oakland: Kaiser Industries, 1968), 18–19.
4. Ingram, (1968), 11–13; (1949), 40–49.
5. *Kaiser*, 27; Ingram, (1949), 51–52; Eliot Janeway, *The Struggle for Survival: a Chronicle of Economic Mobilization in World War II* (New Haven: Yale, 1951), 249; Emory Scott Land, *Winning the War With Ships* (New York: McBride, 1958), 171.
6. Ingram, (1949), 53–55; (1968), 14; Frederic Lane, *Ships for Victory: a History of Shipbuilding Under the U.S. Maritime Commission to World War II* (Baltimore: Johns Hopkins, 1951), 470; United States House of Representatives, Committee on the Merchant Marine and Fisheries, 79th Congress, *Investigation of Shipyard Profits* (hearings, Washington, 1946), 248.
7. Ingram, (1949), 58–59.
8. Janeway, 250.

9. Jack Chambers, oral history, Sausalito Historical Society, 1986; Ingram, (1949), 50; (1968), 17-18.

10. *San Francisco Examiner*, Feb. 6, 1978; *San Francisco Chronicle*, Feb. 6, 1978.

11. Richard Finnie, *Marinship: the History of a Wartime Shipyard* (San Francisco: Marinship, 1947), 45.

12. Chambers, oral hist.; Ingram, (1949), 35, 53; (1968), 6; *Chronicle*, Oct. 19, 1977; *Examiner*, Oct. 19, 1977.

13. Finnie, 4; Chambers, oral hist.

14. Finnie, 5–7.

15. House Committee, 250–251, 504–506.

16. Emory Scott Land, *Winning the War With Ships* (New York: McBride, 1958), 171–173.

17. *New York Times*, Sept. 24, 25, 1946; *Chronicle*, Sept. 27, 1946; House Committee, 373–374.

CHAPTER 3

1. Richard Finnie, *Marinship: the History of a Wartime Shipyard* (San Francisco: Marinship, 1947), 8; Frederic Lane, *Ships for Victory: a History of Shipbuilding Under the U.S. Maritime Commission to World War II* (Baltimore: Johns Hopkins, 1951), 466.

2. Lane, 486.

3. Lane, 1–32; Robert Kilmarx, ed., *American's Maritime Legacy: a History of the Merchant Marine and Shipbuilding Industry Since Colonial Times* (Boulder, Col.: Westview, 1979), 175.

4. Lane, 12–14; Kilmarx, 181. Also see Emory Land's biography, *Winning the War With Ships* (New York: McBride, 1958).

5. Lane, 15, 119–120, 459–463, 788, 794.

6. Lane, 21, 27–28, 40–45; Kilmarx, 175–176; United States Bureau of the Budget, *The United States at War* (Washington, 1946), 136.

7. Lane, 72–100; Kilmarx, 176–177; John G. Bunker, *Liberty Ships: the Ugly Ducklings of World War II* (Annapolis: Naval Institute, 1972), 4-10.

8. Lane, 46–50; Bunker, 12.

9. Lane, 9.

10. Lane, 138–139, 144; Kilmarx, 181.

11. Lane, 147, 133.

12. Lane, 171, 692.

13. Jack Chambers, oral history, Sausalito Historical Society, 1986.

14. Lane, 132–135, 487.

15. United States House of Representatives, Committee on the Merchant Marine and Fisheries, 78th Congress, *Production in Shipbuilding Plants* (hearings, Washington, 1943), 703.

16. Lane, 89-90, 359–360.

17. United States Maritime Commission, press release, Sept. 20, 1943; Lane, 453, 466; *The Marin-er* (Marinship company magazine), Jan. 20, 1945.

18. *Sausalito News*, Apr. 14, 1944; Marin City *Marin Citizen*, Apr. 20, 1944.

19. Maritime Commission, *Report to Congress*, (Washington, 1942), 10; (Washington, 1943), 6.

20. Finnie, 180, 186; *Marin-er*, Aug. 16, 1945.

21. Finnie, 164–166; *Marin-er*, Aug. 16, 1945.

22. Finnie, 186; *Marin-er*, July 7, 1945.

23. Bureau of the Budget, 139; Land, 178.

24. Kilmarx, 186; Lane, 311.

25. Lane, 315, 338; Eliot Janeway, *The Struggle for Survival: a Chronicle of Economic Mobilization in World War II* (New Haven: Yale, 1951), 252.

26. Lane, 333; United States House of Representatives, Committee on the Merchant Marine and Fisheries, 79th Congress, *Investigation of Shipyard Profits* (hearings, Washington, 1946), 250.

27. Maritime Commission, *Report*, (1945), 2.

28. Kilmarx, 189–191; Lane, 117–127.

29. Lane, 487–491, 813–815; House Committee, (1946), 507–510.

30. United States House of Representatives, Committee on the Merchant Marine and Fisheries, Subcommittee on Shipyard Profits, 78th Congress, *Shipyard Profits* (hearings, Washington, 1944); Bureau of the Budget, 140.

31. House Committee, (1946), 1–3; *New York Times*, Sept. 24, 1946.

32. House Committee, (1946), 250–256.

33. *New York Times*, Sept. 25, 1946; *Chronicle*, Sept. 27, 1946.

34. House Committee, (1946), 250.

35. *New York Times*, Sept. 25, 28, 1946.

CHAPTER 4

1. Frederic Lane, *Ships for Victory: a History of Shipbuilding Under the U.S. Maritime Commission to World War II* (Baltimore: Johns Hopkins, 1951), 224.

2. Lane, 202–214; Richard Finnie, *Marinship: the History of a Wartime Shipyard* (San Francisco: Marinship, 1947), 194; Emory Scott Land, *Winning the War With Ships* (New York: McBride, 1958), 169–170.

3. Lane, 206–207; John G. Bunker, *Liberty Ships: the Ugly Ducklings of World War II* (Annapolis: Naval Institute, 1972), 8–9.

4. Lane, 207, 213; Bunker, 13.

5. Lane, 208–210; Bunker, 12; Robert Kilmarx, ed. *American's Maritime Legacy: a History of the Merchant Marine and Shipbuilding Industry Since Colonial Times* (Boulder, Col.: Westview, 1979), 191.

6. Lane, 222–223.

7. *Marinship: the First Two Years* (Sausalito: Marinship, 1944), n.p.

8. Daisy Hollingsworth Edmonds, oral history, Sausalito Historical Society, 1986.

9. Edward Winkler, oral history, Sausalito Historical Society, 1986; Edmonds, oral hist.; *Sausalito News*, Oct, 1, 1942.

10. Edmonds, oral hist.

11. Marin City *Marin Citizen*, Mar. 31, 1944.

12. *Marinship*, n.p.

13. Finnie, 193.

14. Lane, 147, 333.

15. Lane, 203, 332–333.

16. *Marinship*, n.p.; Finnie, 196–197.

17. Finnie, 127–134.

18. Finnie, 196.

19. *The Marin-er* (Marinship company magazine), July 10, 1943.

20. *Marin-er*, Jan. 8, 1944.

21. Finnie, 198.

22. Finnie, 199–200.

23. *News*, Apr. 1, 1943.

24. Finnie, 200.

25. Finnie, 200; *Citizen*, Apr. 14, 1944; *News*, Apr. 20, 1944.

26. Finnie, 200–201; Lane, 681–682.

27. Finnie, 201.

28. *Marin-er*, Jan. 6, 1945.

29. *Marin-er*, Apr. 14, 1945; June 23, 1945.

30. Finnie, 193, 202.

CHAPTER 5

1. Grant Perkins, Mary Entwhistle Poole, oral histories, Sausalito Historical Society, 1986.

2. Moses Beard, Celia Grinner, oral histories, Sausalito Historical Society, 1986.

3. Walter Brown, Dick Miller, Grace Pastori, oral histories, Sausalito Historical Society, 1986.

4. Richard Finnie, *Marinship: the History of a Wartime Shipyard* (San Francisco: Marinship, 1947), 53.

5. Frederic Lane, *Ships for Victory: a History of Shipbuilding Under the U.S. Maritime Commission to World War II* (Baltimore: Johns Hopkins, 1951), 236–237; *San Francisco News*, May 10, 1943; Marin City *Marin Citizen*, April 19, 1943.

6. Finnie, 39–43.

7. *The Marin-er* (Marinship company magazine), Aug. 5, 1944.

8. Finnie, 40; *Marin-er*, July 10, 1944.

9. *Marin-er*, Aug. 5, 1944.

10. Finnie, 58–59; *San Francisco Chronicle*, Aug. 9, 1942.

11. Finnie, 35, 44–45, 244–245.

12. Finnie, 45–53.

13. Finnie, 56–57; *Marin-er*, May 1, 1943, April 28, 1945.

14. *Marin-er*, May 1, 1943, April 28, 1945.

15. Lane, 249.

16. Lane, 239–240, 258–266.

17. Finnie, 40, 60, 205–207; *Chronicle*, Aug. 10, 1942.

18. Finnie, 207–208; Poole, Les Walsh, oral histories, Sausalito Historical Society, 1986.

19. Finnie, 209–210; Poole, Brown, Josephine and Francis Doyle, Ed Vacha, Samuel Knoles, oral histories, Sausalito Historical Society, 1986.

20. Finnie, 94–95, 98–101.

21. Finnie, 96–97; Knoles, oral hist.; *Marin-er*, Feb. 2, 1943.

22. *American Labor Citizen* (San Francisco), April 17, 1944.

23. *Marin-er*, June 10, 1944.

24. Perkins, Vacha, Gerald Carlton, Elizabeth Bronan, oral histories, Sausalito Historical Society, 1986.

25. Perkins, Doyle, oral hists.; *Marin-er*, July 10, 1944.

26. *Marin-er*, Feb. 5, 1944.

27. Perkins, Thelma McKinney, Leon Samuels, oral histories, Sausalito Historical Society, 1986. Probably the largest explosion occurred in October 1943 and destroyed a portion of the publicity office and "rocked" Sausalito. *Sausalito News*, Oct. 28, 1943.

28. Finnie, 74–78, 231–236.

29. Paul Brodeur, *Outrageous Misconduct: the Asbestos Industry on Trial* (New York: Pantheon, 1985), 35, 56, 120, 183; Knoles, Vacha, Gene Perry, oral histories, Sausalito Historical Society, 1986.

30. Lane, 268–278, 288–290, 296–297.

31. *Master Agreement Between the Pacific Coast Shipbuilders and the Metal Trades Department, AFL* (Seattle, 1941), Finnie, 88.

32. *Marin-er*, Aug. 5, 1944, April 3, 1943.

33. Lane, 269, 451–452; *Marin-er*, Sept. 2, 1944; *Chronicle*, April 22, 1942.

34. Finnie, 88–92.

35. *Marin-er*, Feb. 19, 1944; *Bechtel Briefs* (San Francisco), Mar. 1, 1947; Finnie, 211–216.

36. *Chronicle*, May 6, 7, 9, 1943; *San Francisco News*, May 6, 1943.

37. *Chronicle*, May 9, 11, 12, 1943; *San Francisco News*, May 11, 1943; *American Labor Citizen*, May 12, 17, 24, 1943; Finnie, 217.

38. Finnie, 214–215.

39. *American Labor Citizen*, Oct. 25, Nov. 1, 8, 1943.

40. *American Labor Citizen*, Nov. 15, 1943, April 17, June 19, Nov. 6, 1944; *Marin-er*, Sept. 30, 1944; *Chronicle*, June 6, 1943; Finnie, 70–73.

41. Katherine Archibald, *Wartime Shipyard: a Study in Social Disunity* (Berkeley: U. of California, 1947), 130.

42. Archibald, 130, 139, 149–150.

43. Poole, Vacha, Brown, oral hists.

CHAPTER 6

1. Vianne Cochran, oral history, Sausalito Historical Society, 1986.

2. Richard Finnie, *Marinship: the History of a Wartime Shipyard* (San Francisco: Marinship, 1947), 221.

3. William Chafe, *The American Woman: Her Changing Social, Economic and Political Roles, 1920–1970* (New York: Oxford, 1972), 140; Chester Gregory, *Women in Defense Work During World War II* (New York: Exposition, 1974), 81–82.

4. United States Department of Labor, Bureau of Labor Statistics, *Wartime Employment, Production and Conditions of Work in Shipyards* (Washington, Bulletin 824, 1945), 7.

5. Susan Hartman, *The Homefront and Beyond: American Women in the 1940s* (Boston: Twayne, 1982), 21; Chafe, 139.

6. Hartman, 17–18, 21, 78; Maureen Honey, *Creating Rosie the Riveter: Class, Gender and Propaganda During World War II* (Amherst: U. of Massachusetts, 1984), 12; Shema Berger Gluck, *Rosie the Riveter Revisited: Women, the War and Social Change* (Boston: Twayne, 1987), 13.

7. Honey, 21–22; Chafe, 142; Gluck, 11.

8. Finnie, 47.

9. Finnie, 223.

10. *San Francisco Chronicle*, Nov. 8, 1942; *Sausalito News*, Nov. 26, 1942.

11. Finnie, 247, 216–217; Gregory, 55.

12. Finnie, 213–214.

13. Finnie, 53.

14. Finnie, 53, 223–225.

15. Finnie, 221–222.

16. Katherine Archibald, *Wartime Shipyard: a Study in Social Disunity* (Berkeley: U. of California, 1947), 21, 31–32; *Marin-er* (Marinship company magazine), March 6, 1943; Finnie, 247.

17. *Marin-er*, March 3, 1943; Gregory, 86, 88–89.

18. Finnie, 222; Josephine and Francis Doyle, Grace Pastori, oral histories, Sausalito Historical Society, 1986.

19. Finnie, 225–226; *Marin-er*, Dec. 11, 1943.

20. Finnie, 225; Frederic Lane, *Ships for Victory: a History of Shipbuilding Under the U.S. Maritime Commission to World War II* (Baltimore: Johns Hopkins, 1951), 239.

21. Finnie, 222, 225; Hartman, 84; Augusta Clawson, *Shipyard Diary of a Woman Welder* (New York: Penguin, 1944), 15; Eloise Gravis, oral history, Sausalito Historical Society, 1986.

22. Clawson, 165; Gluck, 241; Hartman, 59, 84.

23. Gene Perry, oral history, Sausalito Historical Society, 1986.

24. Finnie, 222, 225; Lane, 257.

25. *News*, Oct. 14, 1943.

26. *Marin-er*, Sept. 16, 1942.

27. *Marin-er*, Feb. 2, 1943.

28. *Marin-er*, May 1, 1943.

29. Finnie, 221.

30. *Marin-er*, Dec. 11, 1943.

31. Lois Banner, *Women in Modern America: a Brief History* (New York: Harcourt Brace, 1974), 206; Gregory, 193–194, 200; Honey, 23.

32. Finnie, 230.
33. Hartman, 24.
34. Chafe, 180; Hartman, 91–93.
35. Hartman, 210, 216; Finnie, 221, *Marin-er*, May 1, 1943.

CHAPTER 7

1. Nathan I. Huggins, Foreword in Douglas H. Daniels, *Pioneer Urbanites: a Social History of Black San Francisco* (Philadelphia: Temple, 1980), xiv–xv.

2. Joseph James, "Profiles, San Francisco," *Journal of Educational Sociology*, November 1945, 168; Cy Record, "Willie Stokes at the Golden Gate," *Crisis*, June 1949, 176; Charles Johnson, *Negro War Workers in San Francisco, a Local Self-Survey* (San Francisco, 1944), 2–4.

3. Shema Berger Gluck, *Rosie the Riveter Revisited: Women, the War and Social Change* (Boston: Twayne, 1987), 23; Susan Hartman, *The Homefront and Beyond: American Women in the 1940s* (Boston: Twayne, 1982), 6, 86; William Chafe, *The American Woman: Her Changing Social, Economic and Political Roles, 1920–1970* (New York: Oxford, 1972), 142; Chester Gregory, *Women in Defense Work During World War II* (New York: Exposition, 1974), 141–142.

4. Johnson, 63; Record, 177.

5. C. L. Dellums, oral history, Regional Oral History Office, Bancroft Library, Berkeley, 1973, 97–99; James, 169; Johnson, 63; Edward France, *Some Aspects of the Migration of the Negro to the San Francisco Bay Area Since 1940* (San Francisco, 1974), 67–68.

6. Richard Finnie, *Marinship: the History of a Wartime Shipyard* (San Francisco: Marinship, 1947), 226, 247; Grace Pastori, oral history, Sausalito Historical Society, 1986; *The Marin-er* (Marinship company magazine), June 26, 1943, Oct. 31, 1943.

7. Leon Samuels, oral history, Sausalito Historical Society, 1986; Davis McEntire and Julia R. Tarnopol, "Postwar Status of Negro Workers in the San Francisco Area," *Monthly Labor Review*, June 1950, 613.

8. Finnie, 39–54.

9. Finnie, 69; Marilynn Johnson, "A Tale of Two Cities: War Housing in the East Bay," unpublished paper presented at meeting of American Historical Association, Pacific Coast Branch, Portland, 1989.

10. *San Francisco Chronicle*, Sept. 19, 1945; Charles Johnson, 20–30; James, 168–173.

11. Samuels, Thelma McKinney, Daisy Hollingsworth Edmonds, oral histories, Sausalito Historical Society, 1986.

12. Gerald Carlton, oral history, Sausalito Historical Society, 1986; Katherine Archibald, *Wartime Shipyard: a Study in Social Disunity* (Berkeley: U. of California, 1947), 59–74.

13. *Master Agreement Between the Pacific Coast Shipbuilders and the Metal Trades Department, AFL* (Seattle, 1941), 4–6.

14. Daniels, 31–42; Robert Knight, *Industrial Relations in the San Francisco Bay Area* (Berkeley: U. of California, 1960), 213, 303, 315, 339, 361; James, 169; Charles Johnson, 18, 70.

15. Thurgood Marshall, "Negro Status in the Boilermakers Union," *Crisis*, March 1944.

16. Record, 177; Charles Johnson, 62.

17. *James v. Marinship*, 25 Cal., 2nd (1945), 726; Charles Johnson, 71.

18. *Marin-er*, Oct. 16, 1942, Aug. 21, 1943; *American Labor Citizen* (San Francisco), Dec. 6, 1943; *People's World* (San Francisco), Jan. 6, 1945.

19. *Marin-er*, Aug. 21, 1943.

20. *Chronicle, People's World, San Francisco Examiner*, Nov. 24, 1943.

21. *Chronicle, People's World*, Nov. 25, 1943.

22. San Rafael *Daily Independent*, Nov. 27, 1943; *Chronicle, Examiner*, Nov. 28, 1943.

23. Moses Beard, oral history, Sausalito Historical Society, 1986; *Examiner*, Nov. 28, 1943; *American Labor Citizen*, Dec. 6, 1943.

24. *Chronicle, Examiner*, Nov. 28, 1943.

25. *American Labor Citizen*, Dec. 6, 1943; *People's World*, Nov. 30, 1943.

26. *Daily Independent*, Nov. 29, 30, 1943; *People's World, Chronicle*, Nov. 30, 1943; *Sausalito News*, Dec. 2, 1943.

27. *Daily Independent*, Dec. 3, 1943; *People's World*, Dec. 4, 1943.

28. *Daily Independent*, Dec. 12, 13, 14, 1943, Jan. 6, 1944; *People's World*, Dec. 12, 14, 15, 1943, Jan. 7, 1944; Marin City *Marin Citizen*, Dec. 17, 1943, Jan. 7, 1944.

29. *Daily Independent*, Jan. 12, 14, 1944; *People's World*, Jan. 13, 14, 1944; *Citizen*, Jan. 21, 1944.

30. Robert Weaver, *Negro Labor: a National Problem* (New York, 1946), 131–152; Neil Wynn, *The Afro-American and the Second World War* (London, 1976), 38–48.

31. United States Fair Employment Practices Commission, press release, San Francisco, Dec. 14, 1943; "Decision on Rehearing, Cases 43, 44, 50, 54," Washington, 1945; *Final Report* (Washington, 1946), 19–21.

32. *People's World*, Jan. 17, 20, 25, 27, 1944; *California Eagle* (Los Angeles), Jan. 20, 27, 1944.

33. *People's World*, Feb. 8, 9, 14, 1944.

34. *Boilermakers Journal* (Kansas City), March 1944, 73–79; *People's World*, Feb. 1, 14, 1944; *Citizen*, Feb. 11, 1944; Weaver, 228–229.

35. *Chronicle, Citizen, People's World*, Feb. 18, 19, 1944.

36. *James v. Marinship*, 731–740, 744–745.

37. *James v. Marinship*, 742, 745. The decision also settled similar cases affecting other Bay Area yards brought after Judge Butler's ruling.

38. *Chronicle*, Jan. 3, 4, 1945; *Citizen*, Jan. 5, 1945; *People's World*, Jan. 3, 4, 5, 6, 1945.

39. Archibald, 92, 96–97.

40. Fred Stripp, "The Relationships of the San Francisco Bay Area Negro-American Worker with Labor Unions Affiliated with the American Federation

of Labor and the Congress of Industrial Organizations," Th.D. thesis, Pacific School of Religion (Berkeley, 1948), 164–169; Weaver, 230; Lester Rubin, *The Negro in the Shipbuilding Industry* (Philadelphia: U. of Pennsylvania, 1970), 50.

41. Beard, oral hist., 1986.

42. Stripp, 166; Record, 177; Rubin, 54.

43. Record, 174–179; McEntire and Tarnopol, 613.

44. Record, 187; *Chronicle*, Sept. 19, 1945, June 16, Nov. 17, 1947, Aug. 29, 1948.

45. James, 176.

CHAPTER 8

1. Alice Phillips Rose, unpublished report to USO-Travelers Aid, San Francisco, 1942.

2. *Sausalito News*, Jan. 14, 1943; Jack Tracy, *Sausalito: Moments in Time* (Sausalito: Windgate, 1983), 159; Josephine and Francis Doyle, oral history, Sausalito Historical Society, 1986.

3. Tracy, 159; *Sausalito Jail Register*, March 1942, Sept. 1942, March 1943; Gene Perry, oral history, Sausalito Historical Society, 1986; Richard Finnie, *Marinship: the History of a Wartime Shipyard* (San Francisco: Marinship, 1947), 44.

4. Finnie, 62; Frederic Lane, *Ships for Victory: a History of Shipbuilding Under the U.S. Maritime Commission to World War II* (Baltimore: Johns Hopkins, 1951), 428–434; W. A. Bechtel Company, Marin Shipbuilding Division, "Problem of Labor, Transportation and Housing for the Sausalito Shipyard of the W. A. Bechtel Company," San Francisco, 1942.

5. Finnie, 62; *San Francisco Chronicle*, May 12, July 27, 1942.

6. *Chronicle*, Aug. 17, 1942; *News*, Jan. 21, Sept. 2, 1943; Marin City *Marin Citizen*, Sept. 8, Oct. 1, 1943; *The Marin-er* (Marinship company magazine), July 16, 1943.

7. Finnie, 66–68.

8. "Marin City," *The Architectural Forum*, December 1943, 67–74; *Chronicle*, July 27, 1942; Mel Scott, *The San Francisco Bay Area: a Metropolis in Perspective* (Berkeley: U. of California, 1959), 253.

9. Finnie, 66–69.

10. Finnie, 69; Bechtel, "Problem"; Scott, 253.

11. Finnie, 64; Walter Brown, oral history, Sausalito Historical Society, 1986; *Marin-er*, March 6, 1943.

12. *Marin-er*, March 6, 1943; Lane, 43; Finnie, 65.

13. Finnie, 64.

14. *News*, Apr. 22, 1943; Scott, 253; Gerald Nash, *The American West Transformed: the Impact of the Second World War* (Bloomington: U. of Indiana, 1985), 74.

15. *Citizen*, July 16, 1943; *Chronicle*, July 27, 1942; Rose, "report."

16. *Citizen*, Aug. 6, 1943; *Chronicle*, May 13, 1943.

116

NOTES

17. As quoted in *Citizen*, Feb. 23, 1945; *Chronicle*, May 16, 1943. Also see "Race Relations on the Pacific Coast," Carey McWilliams Papers, v. 5, Bancroft Library, Berkeley.

18. *News*, Apr. 1, 8, 15, 1943; *Citizen*, July 16, 1943.

19. *Citizen*, Aug. 6, 1943, Feb. 18, 1944.

20. *Citizen*, Jan. 14, 1944; James Bullock and Lanny Berry, *Marin City, USA* (Marin City, 1970), 1–5.

21. *Citizen*, Aug. 13, Oct. 29, Nov. 3, 1943, Dec. 1, 1944, Jan. 26, 1945.

22. *Citizen*, Dec. 10, 1943; *News*, Dec. 30, 1943, May 26, Oct. 20, 1944, June 15, 1945.

23. *Citizen*, Jan. 1, 21, 28, Feb. 4, 11, 1944; *News*, Nov. 9, 1944.

24. *News*, Oct. 15, 1942, March 25, 1943; *Citizen*, Aug. 27, 1943.

25. *Citizen*, Aug. 27, 1943.

26. *Citizen*, Mar. 3, Apr. 28, 1944; *News*, Mar. 18, Apr. 27, 1944

27. *Citizen*, Apr. 21, May 5, 12, 19, 1944.

28. *Citizen*, May 26, Nov. 10, 1944.

29. *Citizen*, July 23, 1943, Jan. 28, Nov. 17, 1944.

30. *Citizen*, Apr. 6, May 18, 1945.

31. *Citizen*, Oct. 6, 1944, May 4, 1945.

32. Leon Samuels, oral history, Sausalito Historical Society, 1986; Persis White and Sarah Hayne, "Marin City: a Social Problem to Marin County," *Immigration and Race Problems* (Oakland: Mills College, 1954), 318–334; Bullock and Berry, 1–5.

33. *Marin Independent Journal* (San Rafael), May 3, 4, 5, 6, 1986; Thelma McKinney, oral history, Sausalito Historical Society, 1986.

34. Rose, "report."

CHAPTER 9

1. Richard Finnie, *Marinship: the History of a Wartime Shipyard* (San Francisco: Marinship, 1947), 370–371.

2. *San Francisco Chronicle*, Apr. 30, 1943.

3. United States Congress, Committee on the Merchant Marine and Fisheries, 78th Congress, *Production in Shipbuilding Plants* (hearings, Washington, 1943), 722.

4. *The Marin-er* (Marinship company magazine), May 29, 1943, June 24, 1944.

5. *Marin-er*, Aug. 20, 1943, Mar. 18, 1944, Mar. 3, 1945.

6. Marin City *Marin Citizen*, Mar. 30, 1945.

7. *Chronicle*, Apr. 28, 1945.

8. *Citizen*, May 25, 1945; *Marin-er*, Apr. 28, 1945; *Chronicle*, May 3, 1945.

9. *Chronicle*, June 29, July 28, 1945; *Citizen*, Aug. 3, 1945.

10. *Chronicle*, Aug. 21, Nov. 1, 1945; *Sausalito News*, Nov. 1, 1945; *Citizen*, Nov. 2, 1945.

11. Finnie, 371.

12. Frederic Lane, *Ships for Victory: a History of Shipbuilding Under the U.S. Maritime Commission to World War II* (Baltimore: Johns Hopkins, 1951), 833.

13. John G. Bunker, *Liberty Ships: the Ugly Ducklings of World War II* (Annapolis: Naval Institute, 1972), 56; Edward Winkler, oral history, Sausalito Historical Society, 1986.

14. Laton McCartney, *Friends in High Places: the Bechtel Story* (New York: Simon and Schuster, 1988).

15. Russ and Gladys Quick, Jack Chambers, oral histories, Sausalito Historical Society, 1986; Robert Ingram, *The Bechtel Story: Seventy Years of Accomplishment in Engineering and Construction* (San Francisco: Bechtel, 1968), and *A Builder and His Family* (San Francisco: Bechtel, 1949); *Chronicle*, Oct. 19, 1977, Feb. 6, 1978; McCartney, 167.

16. Finnie, 370.

17. Harold Vatter, *The United States Economy in World War II* (New York: Columbia U., 1985), 85.

18. Samuel Knoles, Josephine and Francis Doyle, Mary Entwhistle Poole, oral histories, Sausalito Historical Society, 1986; Cy Record "Willie Stokes at the Golden Gate," *Crisis*, June 1949, 175–179.

19. Winkler, Grace Pastori, oral histories, Sausalito Historical Society, 1986; Finnie, 371.

20. Camille Almada, Harold Elberg, Leon Samuels, Gerald Carlton, Walter Brown, oral histories, Sausalito Historical Society, 1986.

21. Almada, oral hist.

Index